O h, that would be tragic," Teri said, automatically falling in line behind Scott. "To wait twenty years to fall in love, only to have it last a month, and then you die."

Scott turned and gave her an "oh, brother" look.

"Come on, Scott!" she teased, swatting at the back of his pack. "Where's your sense of romance?"

"It got tired of waiting around here listening to 'Nature Boy' and ran on ahead of us to the end of the trail." He quickened his pace. "We better try to catch up with it. You wouldn't want me to lose my sense of romance now, would you?"

Teri glanced back at Gordon, who was right behind her. She gave a little shrug and sheepish grin as if to apologize for Scott's comment.

Gordon's intense blue eyes fixed on hers. "I'd wait twenty years," he said just loud enough for her to hear.

Palisades.
Pure Romance.

FICTION THAT FEATURES CREDIBLE CHARACTERS AND

ENTERTAINING PLOT LINES, WHILE CONTINUING TO UPHOLD

STRONG CHRISTIAN VALUES. FROM HIGH ADVENTURE

TO TENDER STORIES OF THE HEART, EACH PALISADES

ROMANCE IS AN UNDILUTED STORY OF LOVE,

FROM BEGINNING TO END!

A PALISADES CONTEMPORARY ROMANCE

WHISPERS

ROBIN JONES GUNN

WHISPERS
published by Palisades
a part of the Questar publishing family

© 1995 by Robin Jones Gunn
International Standard Book Number: 0-88070-755-0

Cover illustration by George Angelini
Cover designed by David Carlson and Mona Weir-Daly
Edited by Janet Koboble

Scripture quotations are from the *New International Version*
©1973, 1984 by International Bible Society
used by permission of Zondervan Publishing House

Printed in the United States of America

For information:
QUESTAR PUBLISHERS, INC.
POST OFFICE BOX 1720
SISTERS, OREGON 97759

95 96 97 98 99 00 01 02 — 10 9 8 7 6 5 4 3 2 1

Wendy Lee Nentwig,

a true friend
with whom I've shared dorm rooms and dreams,
prayers and tears, clothes and friends,
laughter, and my daughter's spelling list.
And that was only the first decade.

But the LORD was not in the wind.
After the wind there was an earthquake, but
the LORD was not in the earthquake.
After the earthquake came a fire, but
the LORD was not in the fire.
And after the fire came a gentle whisper.

1 KINGS 19:11-12

One

Teri Moreno flipped her thick brown hair over her shoulder and peered through the cluster of Maui tourists gathered at the airport baggage claim. She had hoped to see Mark among the locals, but it was her sister's voice that greeted her.

"Teri, over here!"

Anita ran toward her with a lei of white plumeria flowers strung over her arm. "You're here!" Anita said breathlessly, giving Teri a hug. "I'm sorry we weren't here to meet your flight. Here, these are for you." She placed the fragrant flowered leis around Teri's neck. "Dan's parking the car. We got a late start. I'm sorry."

"Don't worry about it," Teri said, lifting the sweet flowers to her nose and drawing in the scent. A dozen memories of her previous summer on the island filled her mind. She looked past her sister and with a sheepish smile asked, "Mark wasn't able to come?"

"No, he'll meet us for dinner, though. You really look great!" Anita said, giving Teri's arm a squeeze. "Did you lose some weight?"

Aware that her slim sister's glance had rested on Teri's thighs, Teri said, "Not really." A familiar uneasiness settled in. She had never been able to wear a size six pair of jeans like her older sister could—nor would Teri ever be able to.

"You look great, too," Teri said. "I love your hair like that. I don't think you've ever worn it that short. It's cute."

Anita fingered the ends of her sleek, dark hair that clung to the nape of her neck. "Do you like it? I had it cut a week ago. I'm still getting used to it, but I think I like it. Dan does."

Just then Dan appeared. He was the same age as Anita, twenty-seven. But his dark, wavy hair and short, stocky build gave him the look of a high school wrestler.

"So how was your flight?" Dan said, giving Teri a hug and motioning with his head that they should follow him to the baggage claim area.

"Fine. Uneventful."

"Don't think for a minute that your five weeks here will be uneventful," Anita said. "We are going to have so much fun! I have all kinds of things planned for us."

Teri wondered if Anita had included Mark in her plans. "That's my suitcase," Teri said.

Dan grabbed it for her and lifted it with ease. He had lots of experience with luggage since he worked as a bellhop at the Halekuali'i, one of the most expensive resorts on the west side of Maui. "Is this your only bag?"

"That's it," Teri said.

"Traveling light this time, I see. Looks like you learned all you need to bring to Maui is a bathing suit," Dan said, leading them out to the parking lot.

"A bathing suit and every hard-earned penny I could scrape up," Teri added. She again drew in the sweet scent of the flowers around her neck as they stepped out from under the protected covering of the baggage claim area. A strong wind blew their hair and dried the perspiration from their shirts.

"Ah!" Teri greeted the island breeze with upturned chin and closed eyes. "It's so wonderful to be back here. Do you know how many times I've dreamed of this very moment? Standing here, feeling this wind in my hair, and smelling the flowers." She impulsively gave Anita a hug. "I can't believe I'm here!"

"Why don't you stay for good this time?" Anita asked.

"Don't I wish," Teri said.

"I'm serious. Why don't you move here?"

"Well, one small matter is making a living on the island."

"They always need teachers," Dan said. "The pay isn't great, but you could always do like the rest of us and wait tables on the weekends."

"I don't imagine the demand is high for Spanish teachers," Teri said.

"We can always find out," Dan replied. He unlocked the trunk of their white compact car and dropped her suitcase inside. It had been a rental car that he had bought from a friend for a low price because the right rear door was smashed in. They still hadn't fixed the door. Teri noticed the rust inside the dented area, which hadn't been there a year ago. She slid into the backseat through the one rear door that did work and made a mental note that, even though they both worked two jobs, they hadn't been able to fix their car. How could she possibly afford to support herself in such an expensive location?

"I don't know," Teri said. "I have a comfortable life in

Oregon. Maui is a great place for a vacation, but I don't know if I could actually live here."

"Sure you could," Anita coaxed her.

Dan paid the airport parking lot attendant and pulled out into the traffic.

"Can you wait for dinner or are you starving? You know it will take about an hour to drive to our side of the island and probably another half hour before we eat," Dan said.

"My stomach can wait," Teri answered. The part of her that couldn't wait was her eyes. They longed to feast on the sights of this enchanted paradise. With all the windows down, Dan drove the two-lane highway that linked the two sides of the island. Anita chattered away as they drove, while Teri only half listened. She was too absorbed in the scenery.

First came the waving sugar cane fields in the central valley. To the left rose Haleakala, the great volcano circled in a wreath of clouds that looked like a halo of baby's breath. The road followed the outer rim of the west side of the island, curving through cut volcanic rock and past sequestered sandy coves shaded by palm trees.

Teri drank in the beauty of the blue ocean and the imposing sight of the nearby neighboring islands, popping up out of the Pacific Ocean: Kahoolawe, Lana'i, and the green, sleeping giant, Moloka'i, which lay only nine miles north of Dan and Anita's small house. She had waited a year in rainy Oregon for this feast of her senses, a year filled with romantic dreams and hope inspired speculations. Now Teri Angelina Raquel Moreno was about to see if those dreams were ready to come true.

"I thought we were going to your house first," Teri said when Dan announced they were almost at the restaurant.

"We don't have time," Anita answered. "Besides, Leilani's is right here, and our house is ten minutes up the road."

"Why can't we go to your house first? What's another ten or twenty minutes?" Teri asked, trying to make her voice sound calm.

"We told Mark we would meet him at the restaurant now. He's probably waiting for us."

"But I'm not dressed for dinner," Teri said, feeling flustered. "I wanted to change."

"For Leilani's?" Anita said. "You're fine. You don't want to look like a *haole,* all dressed up for dinner."

"A what?"

"*Haoli.* That's Hawaiian for 'tourist,' a 'foreigner.'"

Dan added, "It literally means 'stranger.' The locals don't usually dress up. Annie's right; you look fine."

Teri didn't feel fine. She felt scruffy, having been on a plane for more than five hours. Her jeans felt hot, and her white cotton blouse was crumpled. She had wanted to look and feel just right when she saw Mark again and had packed two new sundresses to insure that she did. She felt as nervous now as she had last year when Dan and Anita had set her and Mark up on a blind date.

"Did you take me to this restaurant last summer?" Teri asked, trying to remember what sort of place this was.

"I don't think so. We only went to the one where Danny works."

"Right," Teri said, remembering.

"Leilani's is here at Ka'anapali." Anita motioned out the open window as Dan drove past a lush golf course on the right and turned left into an extensive resort community with beautifully landscaped grounds and a long row of high-rise buildings along the beach.

"This is one of our favorite places," Anita said, smiling at Dan. "When we have a chance to go out, that is."

Dan drove into a parking garage and found a place on the first level. They parked and hurried into the Whaler's Village Shopping Center where dozens of tourists leisurely strolled in and out of the shops.

Teri followed her sister and Dan down the winding cement walkway toward the beach. The closer they came to the restaurant, the more unsure she felt of herself. They took a jog to the left, past several lit tiki torches, to Leilani's Restaurant where Dan opened the door for Anita and Teri.

Teri held her breath. She could feel her heart pounding, not only from the brisk walk but also from the anticipation of seeing Mark.

She remembered feeling caught off-guard the first time they had met. It wasn't that Mark was so perfect looking. He had a broad nose, a wide mouth, and a square jaw. But somehow, all those features together gave him a solid appearance. He didn't open his mouth when he smiled, only the corners curved up. To Teri the expression was mysterious and comforting, a gentle contrast to her own wide smile that showed all her teeth in one flash.

Something had sparked between them at that first glance. Was it love at first sight? She wouldn't go quite that far. But it was definitely fireworks that were strong enough to draw her back to him in her thoughts for twelve long months.

As they entered the restaurant, Teri looked quickly at every person in the waiting area until she found Mark. She fixed her gaze on him as his eyes met hers and his wide lips drew up into a curved smile. But he didn't move.

What is he thinking? Are there fireworks for him? Are there any for me? What am I feeling? I don't even know. Should I go over and hug him? Why isn't he moving?

"There's Mark," Anita said, just noticing him. She forged the way over, and Teri followed.

Mark hugged Anita first, giving her the traditional aloha kiss on the cheek. Then he did the same for Teri. She felt nothing. Everything inside her seemed to have shut down. Could it be that in all the months of anticipation she had built their relationship into something bigger than it was? Now that they were actually back together was Teri experiencing her true feelings, or was she too stunned?

"It's good to see you," Mark said. He was sunburned across the nose. His brown hair had much more blond streaking through it than she had remembered.

"It's great to see you!" Teri said enthusiastically. "How are you doing?"

"Fine. And you?"

"Good. I'm doing really well. It's good to finally be here." *Oh, brother,* Teri chided herself, *I sound like an idiot. Why is this so awkward? It isn't at all like I anticipated it would be.*

The young woman at the hostess desk next to them called out, "Hunter, party of four please. Hunter."

"That's us," Mark said.

"Looks as if we arrived just in time," Dan added, taking Anita by the hand and following the hostess to their table. Mark motioned for Teri to go ahead of him, and he followed the procession.

They had a window seat on the second floor of the restaurant. With no screen or glass to block their path, the balmy night breezes fluttered in off the ocean, which lay only a few hundred yards away.

"Perfect," Anita said, as Dan pulled out her chair. "I love this place. I'm glad you're here, Teri. It gives us an excuse to get out for once."

Mark pulled out Teri's chair. She felt a little silly, as if she and her sister were double-dating to the prom or something.

She studied Mark as he seated himself. She couldn't tell what he was thinking; his face was unreadable. He hadn't promised anything, of course, over the last year. A total of seven phone calls and a few greeting cards between them were the fuel Teri had used to foster and feed her expectations.

"We have to save room for some Naughty Hula Pie," Anita said, glancing at her menu.

Teri opened her menu too, glad to have something to hide behind. She scanned the list of seafood and immediately decided on the mahi mahi. But she kept the menu barricade up and tried to collect her thoughts and feelings. They needed to start talking in a natural manner. That would help. Of course this first meeting would feel tense at the beginning. What had she expected? That he would jump for joy when he saw her? Mark was reserved. She knew that. He was probably just as nervous as she was. If only Dan and Anita weren't there, then everything would feel like it had last summer.

"Have you decided yet? Or do you need a few more minutes?" Their waiter was back to take their order, and Teri couldn't hide behind the laminated paper wall any longer. She lowered it and ordered and then inwardly coached herself to relax.

"So, how's your research going?" Teri asked Mark as soon as the waiter left. Teri knew Mark's work as a marine biologist was a passion in his life. She figured the topic would jump-start the conversation.

"It's going very well. We actually changed our focus to the baby whales. I don't remember if I told you that."

"No," Teri said, smiling and hoping Mark would feel at ease, even if she didn't feel that way herself yet. "You didn't mention that. What are you studying—or researching—then?"

Mark leaned into the table, and speaking to all three of them, he said, "It's basically a study of whales from birth to about one year old."

"And someone is giving you money for that?" Anita asked.

"It's quite important," Mark said. "Did you know that baleen whales are the only whales that are born head first? All the others are born tail first, and so are dolphins."

"And what is the reason for that?" Dan asked.

"No one knows. That's why we're studying it. You see, the birthing process can be several hours long. Since whales are mammals, and of course, breathe air, they could drown if they came out head first. But the baleens are born head first, and they don't drown. It's quite a mystery."

"I just can't believe you're paid to watch baby whales be born," Anita said.

"Have you actually seen one?" Teri asked.

A slow smile pressed up the corners of Mark's mouth as he turned to Teri and said, "Two. I shot some great footage that has been very helpful."

"Let me get this straight," Dan said. "You put on your scuba gear and swim around with a video camera while these baby whales are born, and the mothers don't bother you? I thought they were extremely protective of their offspring."

"They usually are," Mark said. "But Mabel and I are good friends. I've been around her for almost three years so I think it didn't bother her that I was there during the birth. Plus she was pretty busy at the time. I don't think she paid much notice to me. Pua and Nui were there."

"Pua and Nui?" Dan asked.

"Whales," Mark answered, as if he weren't used to having to distinguish between humans and whales in most of his conversations. "They're blue whales like Mabel. Sort of self-appointed aunties. Almost like midwives. It took almost an hour, but little Jonah came out just fine, all twenty-five feet of him."

"And he came out tail first?" Teri asked.

"No, head first. He's a baleen."

"I thought he was a blue whale," Teri said, just as the salads arrived.

"He is. See, there are two basic kinds of whales. Toothed and baleen. Baleens feed on krill. Blue whales are baleens. Actually, three kinds of blue whales are in the rorquals. Mabel's a pygmy blue."

Teri smoothed her salad dressing around and tried not to look as confused as she felt. It was as if Mark were speaking a foreign language.

"The rorquals have that triangle shaped fin on their backs, near the tail." Mark pointed over his shoulder and then looked at Anita and Dan to see if they were following him.

"Oh," Teri said. She broke into a wide smile and said, "I guess I have a lot to learn about whales. All this is new to me."

"It's not really as complicated as I'm making it sound," Mark said.

"I'd like to go out with you sometime," Teri said.

Mark's eyes widened.

"I mean, on your ship, or boat, or whatever you call it." Teri laughed at herself. "I'm such a novice I don't even know what you call it."

"It's a boat," Mark said.

"Well, sometime, when it's convenient, I'd like to go out on your boat and learn more about your great blue, rorqual, baleen friends with the triangle fins on their tails."

"The fin is actually on their backs. By their tails." Mark smiled back. But he didn't extend an invitation for Teri to come out on the boat with him.

She made a mental note of that and brought it up later that

night when she and Anita were alone in the living room.

"Didn't he seem a little aloof to you?" Teri asked. "He didn't ask me to go out on the boat."

"That doesn't necessarily mean anything."

"Yeah, but he seemed so distant, not like I thought he would be. Do you think he's starting to have a hard time relating to humans because he's with whales so much?"

"That's a crazy thing to ask."

"No, it isn't. Mark seems different to me. A lot different than he was last year. Do you think I've changed much?"

"No."

"Then it's he. I think he's emotionally involved with someone else."

"Why in the world would you think that?" Anita said.

Teri could hear the low hum of the ceiling fan as it stirred the night air. "It's just not the same. At all."

"Why are you jumping to conclusions, Teri? You haven't given him a fair chance. One dinner is not enough to throw out your relationship. Didn't you feel anything when you saw him?"

"Not like I did last year. But last year it seemed mutual from the start. I think I was hesitant to let myself feel anything tonight until I knew where he was coming from."

"Maybe he was doing the same thing," Anita said. "You both are making this complicated. You need to wait and see what happens. You'll see him tomorrow."

"I *might* see him tomorrow. Didn't you hear what he said? If the boat stayed in dock he *might* come to the luau. I had the impression that if he showed up at all it would be at the last minute. He sure didn't commit himself to anything, did he?"

"Is that what you were expecting? An instant commitment? Teri, you're analyzing all the romance out of this. You have a tendency to do that, you know. Don't turn this into another Luis relationship."

"It's not," Teri said, instantly on the defense.

"Why don't you sleep on it and see what happens tomorrow? I'm going to bed." Anita gave her a hug before heading off to the bedroom where Dan was already asleep. "Good night!"

Pulling out the Hide-A-Bed and slipping between the cool sheets, Teri wondered if Anita had ducked out so quickly because she didn't want to talk about Luis. Teri curled up and let her mind fill with memories of him. Luis was a terrific man. Everyone thought they would marry. They were from the same backgrounds, had the same major in college, liked the same things, and had dated for almost a year. But one day they looked at each other and mutually decided to end it, even though neither of them could articulate a clear reason either for themselves or for their shocked friends and family.

Teri remembered saying something about how they needed either to marry or break up, but they couldn't go on any longer the way they were. It was too easy, too comfortable, and too unexciting. They were more like two cousins together at summer camp than two people deeply in love. There were no fireworks. Teri needed fireworks.

Since Luis and Teri had broken up during their senior year of college, no other significant man had been in Teri's life. Now, with a glimmer of a relationship with Mark, Teri wondered if her sister were right about her analyzing all the romance out of her relationships. Still, the fact remained: she needed fireworks.

Three

A good night's sleep and a long, hot shower did Teri a world of good. By noon the next day she was feeling much more positive about seeing Mark again. She was ready to settle into the island tempo, to slow down and take things as they came.

The first item that came was the company luau at the Halekuali'i Resort.

"Are we going for the whole day?" Teri asked. "Or do you need to come home and get some work done?" Anita had a home business centered in their one bedroom where she had a small computer set up in the corner. She took in a variety of clerical work, including preparing résumés, translating children's stories into Spanish for a Christian publisher in Arizona, and transcribing medical tapes that arrived in the mail weekly from a large group of physicians in Honolulu. Anita also waitressed on Friday nights at a small restaurant.

"I'm pretty well caught up. I can finish the tapes tomorrow. But I'm going to run into town to FedEx some reports I finished this morning. Do you want to go with me?"

"I think I'll stay around here."

"I'm going to stop by the grocery store, too. We need to take a salad with us to the luau. I'll be back in about an hour, and then we can leave."

Teri busied herself around the house, putting up the Hide-A-Bed, washing the few dishes in the sink, and running the vacuum. In the process, Teri discovered a distinct advantage to the small house Dan and Anita lived in: the cleaning could be done in less than an hour. She settled in on the couch, did some channel surfing with Dan and Anita's tiny old set, and enjoyed feeling warm. Warm and relaxed.

Anita returned and whipped up a tossed salad. Then they were out the door. It was another beautiful day in paradise. Thin white clouds hung over the west Maui mountains, and the ocean glimmered on their left as they drove to the resort.

Halekuali'i sat on a flat peninsula of land on the northern tip of the island. The resort covered more than one hundred acres and had four swimming pools, a private beach, and a five-star rating. Only the elite could afford the luxuries of this "house befitting royalty," which its name meant.

As soon as they turned down the palm tree lined drive that led to the main lobby, Teri felt out of her league. She had a friend back in Oregon who was a millionaire, so it wasn't as if she had never been around anyone who had money. But Jessica never flaunted her wealth. She actually had kept it hidden from Teri and many others for her first few months in their small town of Glenbrooke. Still, Teri knew the difference between those who have it and those who don't. Dan was only an employee here. Teri felt her position was established as well, a visiting relative of an employee.

"Does any of this bother you?" she asked Anita as they pulled down a side road that led into an employee parking area in the back.

"What do you mean?"

"Well, it's all so extravagant here. I don't know if I could work at a resort like this. I'd always feel like a peon."

"I don't feel that way. On Maui it's the *kama'ainas* and the *haoles*. I think we have the advantage being the *kama'ainas*."

"And what is that?"

"*Kama'ainas?* Long-time residents. We're the ones who get to live here, not just visit for a week. So what if we have to work to serve all the tourists? Danny says we're the lucky ones because we'll still be here after they check out. He'll probably still be carrying their bags when they come for a visit next year. And that's the point. Tourists come and go. We stay." Anita parked the car and turned off the engine. "No, I never think of us as peons. We're *kama'ainas*."

Teri wondered if she would feel the same if she ever moved to Maui.

"Can you carry the salad dressing?" Anita asked. "I'll take the towels and the salad. You did bring your bathing suit, didn't you?"

"Of course. It's on under my clothes. I have a feeling I'll be dressing like this for the rest of my visit."

Anita led the way to one of the pools where long tables were set up along a lush lawn under scattered coconut trees. It looked like a scene from a vacation brochure. They added their contribution to the bountiful assortment of salads and set out to mingle with the other employees.

Teri hated this first step at social gatherings, especially when she didn't know anyone. She was by nature an outgoing person and even felt comfortable speaking in front of a group. But making small talk at parties was not her thing.

"Do you want to see where they roast the pig?" Anita asked.

"You're kidding, aren't you?"

"No, they built a special pit. It's called an *imu*. They cook the pigs the old-fashioned way at their weekly luaus here. They call it *kalua*. It's a sort of combination of roasting and steaming. They line the pit with hot stones, and I do mean hot! Then they cover it and insert a bamboo tube so they can pour water in to create the steam. Ours is the most authentic luau on the island."

"I guess so! I suppose we're going to be entertained by hula dancers as well."

"Of course. Fire dancers, too. We get the whole program."

"You're kidding."

"Nope. They treat their employees really well here. And once a year the management throws this big party to let the employees enjoy everything the tourists experience at the luaus. All this for the low admission price of one tossed salad. Not bad, is it?"

Teri shook her head and tried to peer into the steamy pit where the pig was cooking. It was covered with palm branches, and the fragrance that floated toward them was spicy and rich.

"Poor little piggy," said Teri.

"Smells good, doesn't it? They cook it over Hawaiian kiawe wood coals. I told you. It's all authentic." Anita fingered the ends of her short dark hair where it curled at the nape of her neck. "I'm going to find Danny and tell him we're here. He's supposed to get off in about an hour."

Teri noticed a man standing a few yards away by the pool. He was by himself with a can of something in his hand, scanning the crowd as if he were looking for someone. Something vaguely familiar about him made Teri stare.

"Do you want to come with me?"

"No, I think I'll just hang out around here," Teri said.

"Then I'll meet you back here in about twenty minutes. Are you sure you'll be okay by yourself?"

Teri gave her sister a pained expression.

"Okay, okay! I thought I'd ask. I know you don't like this social stuff when you don't know anybody. Here, find a lounge chair by the pool for these towels, will you?"

"Sure," Teri said, accepting Anita's towels and stuffing them under her arm. "I'll find a seat and enjoy the view." She tried hard not to look at the man when she said that.

"Okay. See you."

Teri watched her sister leave and stood there studying the man's every move. No one joined him. No one greeted him. It was as if he were a stranger, a *haole* like she, who didn't know anyone else at this picnic swarming with hotel employees and their friends. Something about him intrigued Teri.

He wore his thick blond hair combed straight back and had the deep, golden tan of a lifeguard with a physique to match. He looked like a strikingly handsome movie star yet at the same time he appeared approachable.

Teri glanced over her shoulder to make sure Anita was gone, and then clutching the towels, she headed for the pool and the mysterious man.

She had a relationship developing with Mark, didn't she? Why did she hope this stranger would notice her?

Teri slowly walked past him. He glanced at her, and she gave him a generic, friendly smile and kept on walking. Now she knew she had seen him before, but she couldn't place where.

Maybe he's a movie star, and he's staying here and just happened to stumble into the employee area.

Teri found two lounge chairs and spread a towel over each of them. She chose to keep her back to the man so she wouldn't be tempted to see if he had noticed her.

"I know you," a deep voice behind her said, causing her to jump.

Teri hadn't heard the man approaching. She turned and looked at him. "Hi."

"I'm sure I know you," he said, "but I can't remember where we've met."

They stood by the lounge chairs, each examining the other. Teri scanned her memory. "I thought you looked familiar, too. But I don't know where we met." Something inside her began to set off sparklers.

"I'm Scott Robinson," he said. "Did we meet in Trujillo?"

"Trujillo?"

"Peru. The excavation site of the Moche warrior priest's tomb?"

Teri couldn't help but laugh. Scott looked surprised.

"I have to tell you," she said, still laughing, "I've heard some pretty creative pick-up lines in my time, but that one wins a prize!"

"I'm serious," he said.

"No, I've never been to Peru," Teri said, trying to suppress her laughter. "I take it you have?"

"About three or four years ago. You remind me of someone who worked there on the archaelogical dig."

"I can guarantee you it wasn't me," Teri said, her smile refusing to go away. "I've been a high school teacher in Oregon for the past three years. I don't even teach archaeology. I teach Spanish."

"Maybe I mistook you for someone else," Scott said, looking apologetic. "It's your hair. A man could get lost in tresses like yours."

Inside Teri a screaming firecracker had been lit and was flying through her head at high speed.

"We must have met somewhere," Teri said, thinking he was about to turn and walk away. "Because you look familiar to me, too. And I know your name, but I don't know from where. I'm Teri. Teri Moreno. Does that ring any bells?"

"Teri," he repeated. He had a rich, smooth, radio- announcer voice. "Teri Moreno." He said it again with his eyes closed, as if he were announcing a contest winner's name. "Teri Moreno!" His eyes snapped open, his face lit up, and he said, "Kelley High, Escondido, California."

"Right! You were on the football team a year ahead of me. Scott Robinson, top scorer at the homecoming game against Vista High."

"And I remember Rick Doyle announcing your name at the year- end assembly when you made cheerleader."

Teri started to laugh again. "Scott Robinson. I can't believe it. I don't think I talked to you once during my high school career, but I sure knew who you were! I have a sister who graduated the same year as you. Anita. She married Danny Romero. Did you know them?"

30

"Danny Romero. I think so."

"They're here. Dan works here at Halekuali'i. I'm visiting them for the summer."

"Amazing," Scott said. "I just started to work here yesterday. I wonder if Dan and I work any of the same shifts. That would be something, wouldn't it?"

Teri noticed Anita coming across the grass toward them. Teri waved and called out, "Annie, over here."

When Anita joined them, she looked at Scott as if perhaps she recognized him as well.

"Hi," Scott said.

Teri cut in. "Don't tell her your name. See if she can figure it out."

"You went to Kelley High, didn't you?"

"That's good for one point," Teri said. "Keep going."

"You were on the football team." Anita looked as if she were trying hard to come up with a name. "And you hung out with Rick Doyle."

"Three for three," Teri said. "Do you remember his name?"

Anita pressed her lips together. "No," she finally said. "I know I should, but eight years is too long for my memory."

"Scott Robinson," he said. "And I remember you. Anita Moreno."

"Anita Moreno *Romero,*" she added. "Do you remember Danny Romero? We were married the summer after we graduated and then moved to Maui. Danny will be here in a little while. I hope you two have a chance to see each other."

"We might actually be working together," Scott said. "I started here yesterday."

"Pretty amazing, huh?" Teri said to her sister. "And get this: before coming here he was excavating some ancient Mayan ruins in Peru. Quite a diversion from the old days in Escondido!"

"Actually, it was Mochica ruins north of Trujillo. And that was several years ago. I sailed here from San Diego with Bob Newcomb. Do you remember him? He was two years ahead of me at Kelley High."

Both Teri and Anita shook their heads. "Too old for me," Teri said.

"I hope you don't think I am," Scott said, looking at her with his soft gray eyes.

Anita cleared her throat and took a step backward. "I think I'll go talk with some of my friends over there. When Danny comes I'll look for you, Scott. I know he'll be glad to see you." Anita excused herself, giving Teri a look that said, *Three's a crowd here.*

Teri felt confused. She couldn't deny or ignore the fireworks that had begun inside her. Though tiny, they were still real. But what about Mark?

CHAPTER

Four

ave you been down to the beach yet?" Scott asked after
Anita left

"No, do you want to go for a walk?" Teri was surprised to
hear herself being so bold, but she didn't want him to leave. She
wanted to keep talking to him, to test the waters and see what
kind of depth might be there. Last night with Mark she had felt
as if they had sailed in shallow waters, and what little of their
relationship did exist was about to crash against the rocks.

"Now who's the one with the pick-up lines?" Scott teased.

"I thought it might be fun to talk. You know, get caught up
on everything, if that's okay with you."

"It's more than okay," Scott said. "Since Bob is the only other
person I know on this whole island, you're a welcome friend."

"You know Dan and Anita," Teri said as they turned and
began to walk together toward the path that led down to the
beach.

"Okay, make that a total of four people."

They strolled along the beach for more than an hour, the

conversation popping back and forth like a ping pong ball at a tournament. Scott told of his uneventful four years at college and how he had graduated with a history major. He had joined a cruise ship for two years and then ended up in Peru where he worked on a dig for almost three years. He returned to California to try to find a use for his college major but had given up. The best course of action seemed to be to sail to the islands with Bob so here he was. They had come on Bob's forty-five-foot sailboat, *Moonfish,* in five weeks with relatively few mishaps.

"Sounds like a great experience. My last eight years haven't been quite as exciting," Teri said and proceeded to tell him about graduating from a Christian college with a teaching credential and moving to Glenbrooke, Oregon, where she had taught for the past three years. "I've been to Mexico on a missions project several times," Teri said. "And I came to Maui for a week last summer. But that's the extent of my world travels."

"Let me tell you," Scott said, "Maui *no ka oi.*"

"I only speak Spanish and English," Teri said. "You'll have to interpret your Hawaiian for me."

"It's a popular saying around here. Haven't you heard it? It means 'Maui is the best.'"

"I'll have to agree with that. I love it here," Teri said. "Peru sounds pretty exciting, though."

They stopped walking and stood side by side, looking out to sea at the white masts of the sailboats skimming across the blue.

"Do you like to sail?" Scott asked.

"I've never been."

"You have to go sailing," he said. "What are you doing Friday morning?"

"I don't know." Teri wasn't sure how to answer what she knew he was about to ask.

"*Moonfish* is docked close by. I can take it out anytime I want. Tomorrow I work, but I'd like to take you out Friday morning."

"Okay," Teri said without hesitation.

"Is six o'clock too early?"

"No, not at all. Do you want me to meet you at the harbor?"

"I can pick you up. Where does your sister live?"

"Napili. Do you know where that is?"

Scott smiled. "That's where I live, too."

They compared addresses and found they were three blocks from each other. "That makes it convenient," Scott said as they headed up the trail back to the group of Halekuali'i employees. "I can tell I'm really going to like it here." He slipped his arm around Teri's shoulders, gave her a little squeeze, and then let go.

She felt warmed and thrilled about the thought of going sailing with Scott Robinson. But then Teri looked up and nearly froze. Mark was standing next to Anita several yards away. He was studying Teri and couldn't have missed seeing Scott hug her.

Oh, no, what is Mark going to think? And what is Scott going to think when I introduce him to Mark?

Scott noticed Anita right away and said, "Is that Dan standing next to Anita?"

"No, that's Mark Hunter. He's a marine biologist who lives on a boat docked in Lahaina. You two might have a few things in common, that is if you've ever seen a whale up close."

"Many times," Scott said.

They were now a few feet away, and Scott smiled at Anita and then stuck out his hand to introduce himself to Mark. "I hear you know a thing or two about whales," he said.

"I guess you could say that," Mark said. He glanced at Teri.

"Did Anita tell you we went to school with Scott?" Teri hoped Mark wouldn't view this as what it was. Then she wished he would see Scott as competition so that he would establish where he was. Did he want a relationship with Teri or not?

"Is Dan around?" Scott asked.

"He's playing volleyball with some other guys over there," Anita said.

"Do you mind pointing me in the right direction?"

Anita looked at Scott and then at Teri and Mark. Teri tried to give her a subtle message that said, *Please let me be alone with Mark. Please leave with Scott.*

"I was just heading that way," Anita said. "Do you want to come with me?"

"Sure." Scott turned to Teri. He gave her a look that was more tender than a woman would receive from someone who was merely an old acquaintance. "I'll see you later," he said and followed Anita to the volleyball court.

"So, you were able to make it," Teri said to Mark once they were alone. She walked a few feet over to the lounge chairs where their towels were still draped across the back and sat down. She hoped she was coming across casual and natural and not as mixed up as she felt.

Mark sat in the chair next to her and didn't say anything.

"Isn't this a beautiful resort?" Teri said, trying to get the conversation going.

Mark nodded.

"Do you know when they're going to start eating?"

"Pretty soon."

"Good," Teri said. "That's good." *Oh, dear, this conversation is going nowhere. What happened? Last summer we really clicked. I don't understand what's going on here.*

"I need to get back in a little bit," Mark said. "I suppose I'll see you at church on Sunday."

Teri drew in a breath and said, "Sunday?" Why was Mark waiting so long to see her again? She had planned to spend all her time with Mark. But, of course, now her attention was divided with Scott in the picture. Sunday was four days away. She might be able to figure things out by then, especially if she spent some time with Scott on Friday.

"Okay, Sunday," she agreed.

They made small talk for another ten minutes. It felt stilted and uncomfortable.

"I guess I'll be on my way," Mark said after one of several awkward pauses. "Well, I'll see you later." He smiled as he rose and said, "See you Sunday."

Closing her eyes and releasing a heavy sigh, Teri prayed silently, *Father, what is going on here? Nothing is happening the way I thought it would. What's with Mark? And why is Scott suddenly entering my life? I don't know what you're trying to do. I didn't come here on a manhunt. Or did I? I feel as if I'm acting like a teenager. My emotions are a mess. Maybe neither of these men is right for me. Oh, Father, just show me what you want me to do, okay?*

Before she could whisper "amen," Teri felt a splash of ice on her bare leg. She jumped and let out a squeal of surprise.

"Whoa, sorry there!" a man said as he tried to scoop up the ice cubes and put them back in his plastic cup. Sticky Coke dripped down her calf and soaked through the beach towel.

"I wasn't watching where I was going," he said with a definite accent. Australian, perhaps.

"That's okay," Teri mumbled, flicking the melting cubes onto the cement.

"If you don't mind my saying so, it almost looked as if you were praying," the man said.

Teri looked up at him, shielding her eyes from the sun with her arm, and answered, "I was."

His face, which was tanned and lined like a trapper's or an explorer's, wore the look of someone who had confronted a lion and walked away. He was older than Teri by quite a bit, she guessed. His brown hair was parted on the side, but a few maverick strands fell across his broad forehead. It was hard to determine his eye color because his eyes squinted when he smiled, revealing crows' feet that stretched to his temples. And that's what he was doing, smiling at Teri as he stood over her.

"Gordon," he said, extending a hand to Teri. "Gordon Allistar. Nice to meet you."

Teri didn't know what to make of this guy. Did he spill the Coke so he could introduce himself?

"And what's your name?" he asked, sitting down next to her as if he had been invited.

"My name?" Teri couldn't help but tease this jovial fellow. "Sorry, it's unlisted. So is my phone number."

Gordon let out a hearty laugh. Teri wondered if people were staring at them, his laugh was so loud. But she couldn't help smiling in response. When he laughed, his very soul seemed to participate in the event. His eyes squeezed shut, and his cheeks puffed up. He looked like a three-year-old in the middle of a tickle war.

"I take it you aren't accustomed to being 'picked up,' as they say."

"No," Teri said as firmly as possible.

Gordon rose to leave. Teri felt proud of the way she had handled this pick-up artist. He gave her a slight wink and said, "You could very well be the one."

"The one what?"

He strolled past her, his crazy smile still lighting up his face. All he said was, "Until."

"Weirdo," Teri muttered, glancing around her to see if other people were watching. They weren't. At least not obviously. She kept her eyes on Gordon as he returned to the open bar and stopped to talk to the bartender.

She was still scrutinizing his every move when Anita and Dan returned with Scott.

"Did Mark leave?" Anita asked.

"Mark? Oh, yeah. Mark. Yeah, he left." Teri focused in on Scott and shook the experience with the strange Australian from her mind. "Are we about ready to eat?"

"Yes, that's why we came to get you," Anita said. "Are you all right? You look kind of spooked."

"Me? Oh, no, I'm fine. Some jerk spilled his Coke on my leg, that's all." She turned to Scott and said, "So, do you remember Dan from Kelley High?"

"Yeah, we were in wrestling together," Scott said. He was so tall she had to look way up at him. He was certainly one handsome, powerful looking man.

Dan and Anita started to reminisce about the Kelley High Cougars, and Scott offered Teri a hand so she could stand up.

She accepted it and stood. Then feeling self-conscious at his touch, she let go.

The four of them walked toward the food line. On an impulse, she turned and looked over her shoulder, back at the bar. Gordon was still standing there, only instead of talking to the bartender, he was leaning on one arm, watching Teri's every move. When he saw her look at him, he lifted his refilled glass of Coke in a toast to her.

I can't believe this! I feel as if I've stepped into a rerun of "The Love Boat." Three attentive men in the same day. Well, take Mark off the list and make that two attentive men. One nut case from down under and one incredible man standing right next to me.

Five

❦

"I really should go," Scott said, rising from the table on Dan and Anita's patio. "This has been a great day. And can you believe we're practically neighbors?"

Teri knew it must be close to midnight. They had been having so much fun she didn't want the day to end. The four of them had stayed together for the entire luau at Halekuali'i. They had sat on woven mats and had eaten the roasted pig off of some kind of huge leaves. Dan and Anita had treated Scott and Teri as if they were a couple who were visiting their island, even instructing them on how to eat the traditional *poi* by scooping the gray, pasty food up with two fingers. Then came the hula dancers, which included the *kahiko,* or ancient hula dances, and then the Tahitian fire dancers. At sunset came the blowing of the conch shell and the lighting of the tiki torches.

They had ended up returning to Dan and Anita's for coffee and more talking. Anita had pulled out her old yearbooks, and the four of them took turns telling high school stories. Teri noticed that she and Scott knew many of the same people, and yet in high school their paths never had crossed.

Scott stood and stretched. He still carried himself like a football star, although his face was now that of a man. In the yearbook pictures he had looked like a tough kid trying to prove something.

"I'll see you at work tomorrow, Dan," he said. "And again, the invitation is open, Anita. If you want to come sailing with Teri and me on Friday, you're welcome to join us."

"No, I really need to work. Thanks anyway."

Scott turned to Dan. "We'll have to find a time when we all have the day off. I'd love to take all of you out on the *Moonfish.*"

"That's going to be pretty tricky," Dan said. "I've been saving all my vacation time for a camping trip. We're hiking through Haleakala, the volcano, in two weeks. I've waited two years to get reservations."

"Reservations for what?" Scott asked.

"Some cabins are inside the crater. Three of them. They were built in the thirties, and they hold twelve people. Over the past few years they've become so popular, the park service holds a lottery to draw names to decide who gets to stay in a cabin. My name was drawn this year."

"You have to be kidding," Scott said. "You mean you can hike into the crater?"

"Yep. They say it's unlike any other place you've ever hiked. A bunch of us at work have been entering the lottery off and on for the past two years. Believe me, nothing is going to stop me from going on this backpack!"

"Are all twelve places taken?" Scott asked.

"They are at this point. Would you like to get on the list if anyone drops out?"

"Yeah!" Scott nodded and looked as if Dan had offered him tickets to the Super Bowl. "Put my name down. I'm in the second one of your buddies drops out."

"No problem," Dan said. "I'll check around at work tomorrow."

"I'll be there," Scott said. "Keep me posted." He turned to Teri and said, "And we have a date Friday morning on the *Moonfish.*"

Teri smiled. "I'll see you then!"

Scott let himself out. Dan and Anita both stared at Teri.

"What?" she said.

"This is pretty interesting," Dan said. "You have Mark on the line and Scott in the net. I didn't know you were into competitive fishing."

"Oh, right! Like I really went out searching for Scott. We happened to bump into each other. I went to high school with him, too, you know."

Anita looked concerned. "What are you going to do about Mark?"

"What do you mean? Why do I need to do anything about Mark? He said he would see me on Sunday. So, I'll see him on Sunday. In the meantime, I'll go sailing with an old friend on Friday. Are there any ancient Hawaiian laws that say I can't do that?"

"I think you need to talk to Mark before you go sailing," Anita insisted.

"Why?"

"So you know where you stand with him."

Dan listened to the two with a cat grin on his face.

"I don't know that I *want* to know or that I *need* to know where I stand with Mark," Teri hotly replied. "He's not a very talkative person, in case you hadn't noticed."

"All the more reason for you to be up front with him," Anita said. "He saw you with Scott today. We both saw Scott give you a hug when you were coming up from the beach. What is Mark supposed to make of that?"

"Why does it matter to you what Mark makes of it?" Teri spouted back. "Can't I take things as they come? This is my life we're discussing here, remember? What difference is it to you if I want to go out with two men in the same week? That is, if you want to call dinner last night a date. It seemed more like you two were babysitting Mark and me. Maybe I need to be alone with Mark once to see what's really there. And maybe I need to be alone with Scott once to see if anything is there. It's kind of hard for me to discover such things when you guys are always around."

"Well, excuse us!" Anita said, pushing herself away from the patio table and marching inside. "You want to be alone? Fine. I'll leave you alone. Good night!"

Teri heaved an angry huff. Why did she and Anita relate this way? Either they were intensely connected, like two eyes looking out of the same head, or they were complete opposites who saw everything differently.

"You two drive me crazy," Dan said after a moment. "I've never known two people who could be so identical and so opposite at the same time."

"She just wants to run my life," Teri said. "We would get along great if she didn't always have to be my boss. Or my mother. Or whatever it is she's trying to be."

"She's trying to be a big sister."

"Why can't she just be my *sister,*" Teri said, looking up and searching Danny's expression for an answer. "She is only fourteen months older. Why does she always have to try to dominate me?"

"I don't know. Birth order, I guess. Why do you always have to be so defensive?"

Teri threw his logic right back at him with a casual, "Oh, birth order I guess."

"You probably don't want to hear this," Dan said, "but may I offer a little big brotherly advice?"

Teri shot him a wary glance.

"Take it slow, Teri. From what I know of Mark, he's level-headed, is a strong Christian, and has a good reputation. All I know about Scott is what's left over of his high school reputation. You and I both know it wasn't the greatest. So, if things start moving quickly with Scott, will you do me a personal favor and take it easy until you know him better?"

Teri didn't answer. She didn't like Dan lecturing her, especially after Anita's mothering comments. But she didn't want to be a brat, either. She wanted to be clear-headed and unemotional and take in her brother-in-law's advice like a mature, twenty-six-year-old woman. Unfortunately, she felt about thirteen.

"God has the right man for you, Teri," Dan said as he rose to leave. With a yawn he opened the sliding glass door and added, "Just be patient and wait for the right one."

Teri had waited. While she waited, she had watched Anita and Dan's love affair for ten years. Of course Dan could say, God has the right man for you. He and Anita met when they were high school freshmen. They fell in love and were married two weeks after graduating from high school. Neither of them knew anything about blind dates or sitting home alone weekend after weekend. Neither of them knew the pain of breaking up with someone after dating him for almost a year.

Teri swished the cold coffee grounds around in the bottom of her cup. She was irked whenever anyone used pat Christian answers to explain something in life that was difficult. "God is in control." "God will work it out." "Wait on the Lord." Teri knew them all. And she knew that, while they held important truths, many times they had been reduced to a simple reply to a complex situation.

Teri also had to admit that she had used those statements herself on countless occasions. Both she and Anita had learned them growing up as daughters of the pastor of a large Hispanic church in north San Diego County. But the older Teri became, the harder she found it to explain the disappointments in life. She couldn't believe a capricious God would choose to bless some people in their love lives and ignore others.

Glancing at the night sky, she noticed dozens of stars twinkled down on her, all winking. "Okay," she whispered into the stillness, "I'm waiting."

The next morning, Teri and Anita acted as if they had not had a tiff the night before. Anita wasn't feeling well, which put her more in the mode of a kitten than a tiger. She worked quietly in her room, and Teri entertained herself reading out on the patio, or "lanai," as Dan and Anita called it, and then watching some television. Finally she decided to act on her goal to exercise every day of her vacation. She had procrastinated long enough.

"I'm going for a walk," Teri called out through Anita's closed door. "If I'm not back in an hour send out the hound dogs."

Anita didn't answer. Teri quietly opened the bedroom door and spotted Anita curled up on her bed fast asleep. Her computer was on. It looked as if the past few late nights had caught up with her. Teri tiptoed over to the desk, wrote a note on a Post-It, and stuck in on the computer screen. Then she left the room and closed the door.

Outside half a dozen barefoot kids were playing in the street. The sky over them hung heavy with thick, pink clouds streaked with white strips of sunlight. Teri walked out of the cul-de-sac and headed toward the beach.

She knew it was more than half a mile down to the sand, but she didn't care. She was on Maui. What was a mile's walk to the beach and back? In Oregon it took her more than two hours to drive to the coast, and once she arrived, the temperature was so cold she couldn't stand to walk barefoot in the sand. Maui's warm sands beckoned her feet to come to them this beautiful afternoon, and she would oblige.

The wind kept her company as she made long strides through the housing development and downhill toward the highway. In front of her, majestic Moloka'i, the neighboring island, rose in great, green splendor. It looked so close, as if she could swim right over to it.

She had heard of wind surfers skittering the nine miles across the Pailolo Channel from Maui to Moloka'i on a windy day. She wondered if any were trying the journey today. It seemed windy enough from where she was standing.

When Teri crossed the main road, the wind decreased markedly, blocked by continuous buildings—condominiums, hotels, motels, resorts. They looked like one long barricade that not only cut the wind but also blocked Teri from the sand.

She walked through the grounds of one of the motels and headed out to the beach. Slipping off her sandals, she twisted her toes into the warm, white sand. Closing her eyes, she savored the moment.

Then, instead of walking along the shore, Teri found a spot to settle in the sand. She watched the dozens of people. A few feet to her right, a father with a belly that hung over his swim trunks was barking commands to two little kids who were trying to ride a gentle wave into shore on a Styrofoam surfboard. The little girl looked as if she were close to tears as her dad said, "Come on, do it again! This time look up at the camera and wave to Daddy. That's it! Go catch that wave, honey."

A woman in front of Teri wore a tiny bikini. Her skin was deep red. She lay on her stomach with sunglasses on, elbows propped up, as she read a thick novel. Teri noticed she was turning the pages fast, as if she had to finish this book by a certain time.

Couples strolled by, and toddlers squatted at the shore and scooped wet sand with blue plastic shovels. Everyone seemed so busy vacationing, so hurried about their relaxing. Teri promised herself she would downshift. She would take everything at a much slower pace and savor every moment.

She tried not to think about getting married, about sitting on a beach someday watching her own children play. But it was hopeless. The sights and sounds of families, of children, of couples, surrounded her.

Funny, but she didn't feel lonely like this when she was working. Her life in Glenbrooke was full and rich. So far this vacation, which was supposed to help her relax and become rejuvenated, had only brought confusion about Mark and longing for marriage. It was not a satisfying combination.

Teri took her time walking back. She knew the answers to her heart's questions were not simple ones. Marriage to the right man didn't insure happiness and the coming true of all one's dreams.

Even her sister had struggles. Twice Anita had miscarried. Several years had passed since she had lost the last baby, and Teri knew Anita was afraid to try again.

How much better it would be, Teri thought, *if I could learn to be content in whatever my situation.*

Resolved to discover a deeper level of contentment, Teri concentrated on smelling the flowers on her walk back to the house. She listened for every bird and toyed with the idea of moving to the island permanently. Today the thought seemed like a good one.

Her laid-back mood matched the day when she met Scott the next morning. The drive down to Maalaea Harbor was beautiful, and Teri breathed in the sights, sounds, and scents along the way.

"I think I could live here," she said.

"I have plans to stick around quite awhile," Scott said. "I wouldn't mind a bit if you were part of those plans."

Teri hadn't expected those words. What was Scott thinking? They had only met a few days ago.

"Are you going to try to get a job here?" Scott said.

"Well, I don't know. I hadn't thought that far ahead."

"I've been thinking pretty far ahead these past few days," Scott said. "Funny thing is, every thought seems to have you at the center."

Teri didn't glance over at him. She wasn't sure how to take his comments.

"Here we are," Scott said, pulling into the harbor. "You're going to love the *Moonfish*. Can you grab the towels in the backseat? I'll get the ice chest and the bag of gear out of the trunk."

Teri followed Scott to the dock where he pointed out the sleek, white sailboat. "There she is. Isn't she a honey?"

The boat looked pretty ordinary to Teri, but then she wasn't sure what she was supposed to be looking for. "I can't believe you sailed all the way here from San Diego on this little boat."

"Lots of people have made the crossing in smaller vessels than this."

"Is the moonfish the name of an actual fish?" Teri asked as they boarded.

Scott offered her a strong hand and said, "Yep. They're a long, thin fish with a silvery body. The first time I ever saw one was in Peru. They have great big eyes and a funny, upturned mouth."

"I've never heard of them," Teri said. But then, she knew little about marine life in general. She had discovered that quickly enough when Mark talked about whales.

Thinking about Mark gave Teri a funny feeling. The ocean was Mark's domain, yet Teri was going out to sea with another man. It felt strange. For an instant Teri wondered if by some bizarre chance they might run into Mark out on the water.

"Here, hold this, will you?" Scott said, lifting up a thick rope. "I'm going to need some help getting out of the harbor. I'll just tell you what to do and do it as quickly as you can, okay?"

"Aye, aye, captain."

Scott smiled at her humor, and as he passed her, his arm brushed against her shoulder. Teri couldn't help but wonder if he had noticed the magnetism between them. It intrigued her and enticed her yet made her feel a little frightened.

For the next twenty minutes, Scott called out his commands, trying his best to give Teri a crash course on the anatomy of a sailboat and how to handle her. They made it out to the open sea with no problems. Soon they were skimming across the deep blue water with salty spray clinging to their arms, legs, and faces. "You're right," Teri called out over the roar of the wind, "I love it!"

Scott smiled back, looking pleased. He had been busy unfurling the sails, pulling a rope here, winding something over there.

"Do you want to ride the winds some more?"

"We can slow down," Teri called back. "Let's kick back for awhile."

Scott relinquished his battle to harness the ferocious wind and let the taut sails relax. Almost instantly the boat slowed, and everything around them seemed quiet. They were still moving, bobbing about, and the wind was still blowing through Teri's hair. But it was calmer. Slower. The way she wanted her time on Maui to be.

"Hungry?" Scott said. He moved over to where Teri sat toward the front of the *Moonfish*. She had been using the ice chest for a footrest.

"A little thirsty," she said, shifting her position so Scott could open the chest.

"Raspberry or cherry?" he asked.

"Raspberry sounds good." When he handed her a wine cooler, she asked, "Do you have anything else in there?"

"No, just raspberry and cherry."

"I meant like juice or soda. I don't drink alcohol."

Scott looked at her as if he couldn't believe what he had just heard. "Why not?"

"Well, because, I just don't. I never have."

"Never?"

"No. Never."

"You've never had a beer?"

"No."

"A glass of wine or champagne? Not even at a wedding?"

"No. Never."

"Then how do you know you don't like it?"

"I didn't say I didn't like it. I just don't drink."

"But why?" Scott asked, flipping the lid on his bottle and taking a swig.

Now Teri was stumped. No one had ever challenged her like this before. In high school, when she was offered alcohol, she had plenty of reasons that most of her friends respected—her parents forbade it, she was under age, or she was a Christian and therefore didn't drink. Now the only reason that applied was being a Christian. Yet she had lots of Christian friends who drank, and they seemed to have strong relationships with God.

"It's a personal choice. It's not right for me because I'm a Christian. Not that Christians can't drink in moderation if they want to, but I don't. At all. It's my choice."

Scott tilted his bottle in a toast to her. "A woman of virtues," he said. "Even more reason for me to keep you around. You could turn out to be a good influence on me."

Then, before Teri knew what was happening, Scott leaned over and kissed her on the lips.

Seven

T hen what did you do?" Anita asked, staring at her sister as she related the morning's events.

"At first I froze. I couldn't move. I could hardly breathe! Then he moved closer to kiss me again, and I pulled away."

Anita waited. She was dressed for her waitress's job in a white shirt and black skirt and looked a bit like a lawyer.

"I told him it was all happening too fast, and I needed to take things slower. He said he liked that in a woman and then finished his wine cooler."

"That was it?" Anita said. "Nothing else happened?"

Teri paused. "No, we just talked for about an hour or so, and then we put the sails back up and sailed home. He asked me to dinner Sunday night."

"And you said yes?" Anita asked.

"Of course I said yes."

Anita looked up at the kitchen ceiling and shook her head.

"What?"

"You trust him?"

"Of course I trust him! Why shouldn't I? He respected me today. He even called me a woman of virtue because I didn't drink. Why shouldn't I go out with him again?"

"Teri, will you turn on your brain? This is Scott Robinson we're talking about here."

"What are you saying? That I'm not good enough for a man like Scott Robinson?"

"Good enough? You're too good! The guy is a smooth operator. He's coming on to you, and you're playing right along every step of the way. I can't believe this. I absolutely can't believe this! Especially when you have a relationship already going with Mark Hunter. Now there's a man of virtue."

"Then how come this man of virtue hasn't called since I've been here or asked me out?"

"Probably because he saw you with Scott at the luau. I told you that you needed to talk to him." Anita looked smug.

Teri hated it when her sister acted superior. "It's really not up to you to decide whom I should go out with," Teri said with a snap in her voice. She rose from the kitchen stool where she had been sitting, ready to march off. The problem with a small house was that it didn't offer many places to march off to.

"Just answer one question for me," Anita said, raising her voice. "Since when did you start going out with men who weren't Christians?"

Teri spun around. "You can't tell me Scott isn't a Christian."

"Oh, is he?"

"You heard him the other night when he was here. He went to church with Rick Doyle and those other guys when he was in high school. Then in college he sort of floated away from church. He said he's coming back now, and he still believes everything he did in high school."

"That's a long time to float," Anita said.

"You know what your problem is? You're too judgmental," Teri said.

"Oh, really? Well I'd love to stand here and debate the point with you, but I have to go to work. We'll finish this discussion later, Teri."

"You're not my mother!" Teri shot back at Anita as her sister swished out the front door. The door slammed shut, and Teri released a frustrated "Grr!" It was ridiculous to fight with her sister like this.

Teri figured that, because she and Anita had been so close when they grew up, they had developed set patterns of interacting with each other. After Anita had moved to Maui, they had little chance to see each other. The two didn't know how to relate to each other as adults.

Teri stormed over to the refrigerator and looked for something to drink. She settled on a bottle of sparkling water. Raspberry. It looked similar to the bottle of raspberry wine cooler Scott had offered her that morning.

Why couldn't Scott have brought along some sparkling water? That might have eliminated their conflict right from the start. Flipping off the lid, Teri retreated to the lanai.

The covered porch was separated from the dining area by a sliding glass door. Beyond the lanai, hibiscus bushes were thick with red, trumpet-shaped flowers, and a plumeria tree blossomed nearby. The profusion of vegetation provided a solid green barrier from the nearby neighbors and a beautiful view out the sliding glass door. This evening the hibiscus plants were releasing their subtle fragrance into the soft breeze.

Teri had lied to Anita. Well, not actually lied. She had made the incident on the sailboat appear harmless, as if everything had been smoothed out. It had ended that way, but what Teri had omitted from the version she had told Anita was the disagreement she and Scott had not managed to resolve.

Teri hadn't felt she could tell Anita the details of her encounter with Scott. Anita would only lecture her, and she didn't need that now. Not at all. What she needed was time to think, to sort things out. She was glad that both Dan and Anita were working at their restaurant jobs tonight. She needed to be alone.

Now, in the cool of the evening as Teri sat on the lanai, she tried to figure out what had happened between her and Scott. When he was about to kiss her the second time, Teri had pulled away and had said, "This is happening too fast, Scott. Can we take things slower?" It wasn't until nearly twenty minutes later that he had said he liked that in a woman and then had finished his wine cooler.

After she had told him things were going too fast for her, he had invited her to sit down so they could talk. She had sat across from him, on top of the small ice chest, with her hands folded across her stomach.

Teri had told him she didn't like being taken advantage of and she felt that was what he was trying to do. Scott had become defensive and had said she really needed to lighten up, that she was too rigid.

"I know your dad is a pastor and you grew up with these standards. I think it's great. Really!" Scott had said. "But I guess what bugs me about some Christians is that they are so locked into their worldview that they don't have a clear understanding of reality. They think everyone should be like them, but not everyone is. They disassociate themselves from the rest of the world, sit back, and condemn everyone else for not being like them."

"I'm not like that," Teri said.

"I'm not saying you are. I'm only saying it's something to think about. Your standards are great. Admirable. Honorable, even. It's just that the rest of the world isn't exactly of the same mindset."

"Well, it should be," Teri spouted and then immediately wished she hadn't been so blunt. Her response had been exactly what Scott was saying: biased, judgmental, rigid. "I mean, it would be a much safer world if people had higher morals. Don't you think?"

"Sure. But I just think you shouldn't expect everyone in the world to live by your rules."

"Now you're the one who's being judgmental!" Teri responded. "Christianity isn't based on a bunch of rules. It's a living, growing relationship with Christ."

"And all the rules your Christian leaders have imposed on you, like not drinking."

Teri didn't answer right away. Scott had a point. "I guess I need to think that one through. I'm still in the process of deciding what's right for me."

"Then have a wine cooler with me. How can you decide unless you try both sides?"

"I don't want one," Teri said.

"Why not?" Scott sounded irritated.

"I need to think all of this through some more," Teri said defensively. "Can't you grant me a little time and space to do that?"

"Sure." Scott gave her a tender look. "We have time. Take all you need."

Teri released her tight grip across her stomach. She tilted her chin up and let the wind blow the curls off her forehead.

Scott smiled at her. "I like it that you have strong morals and are zealous about what you believe. You could actually be a good influence on me. And who knows, I might even have a little influence on you."

Why had Scott said she could be a good influence on him? Did he, the man who had traveled the world, need straightening out? What kinds of things had he experienced? What had caused him to waiver from his Christian beliefs, and what was it that was bringing him back now? Was he right that she was too rigid? Did she judge others by an unfair and unrealistic standard? Had she lived dependent on a set of rules that needed realignment?

Instead of coming up with answers, all Teri had was an empty stomach. Suddenly she realized she wanted pizza, and she wanted it now. Setting aside her troubled thoughts about Scott, wine coolers, kisses, and rules, she found the phone book and looked up the name of a pizza shop that advertised free delivery.

"Yes, I'd like Canadian bacon, pineapple, and olives on that."

"Okay. We're looking at about half an hour. I need your name and address."

Teri provided the information and hung up thinking, *I can't wait half an hour!* She scanned the refrigerator again in hopes of finding something she could chomp into. The fridge held half a papaya, some leftover salad, a loaf of bread, and seven eggs. In the bottom bin she found a carrot and decided that was about as good as she could do in the chomping department.

She tried to watch TV while she waited. As soon as the first program ended, she checked the clock. It had been almost half an hour since she had called. What was taking them so long?

The next program began and successfully dulled her senses for another half hour. Now she was ticked. What was the problem? She went to the phone and began to flip through the phone book in search of the pizzeria's number when the doorbell rang.

Teri stomped to the door muttering, "It's about time." She jerked open the door and found herself face to face with the man who had spilled Coke on her at the luau.

He looked as surprised to see her as she was to see him. He glanced at the slip of paper taped to the top of the pizza box as a huge smile lit up his face.

"Teri," he said in his brisk Australian accent. "Your name is Teri, then is it?" He started to laugh with wild, total abandonment, and Teri wondered if the neighbors might be peeking out their windows to see what was going on.

"How much do I owe you?" she said flatly, not at all thrilled that this peculiar person now knew her name.

"Ten fifty-seven." He seemed to study her face as she fished in the bottom of her purse for the right change. "Annie's sister, right?"

Teri looked up, surprised that he knew Anita. However, this was a small community. Perhaps Dan and Anita ordered pizza from him before. She gave an obligatory nod and held out the money for him. She had included a dollar tip.

"Great! Thanks, Teri," he said, taking the money and handing her the pizza box. He didn't move but stood there grinning at her.

"Okay, well, thanks," Teri said. She edged the door closed a few inches. He still stood there, looking as if he might burst into his jolly laugh all over again. "Is something wrong?" she asked pointedly, staring back at him.

"Not a bit. Everything's as right as right can be." Still he didn't move.

"Good." Then using his word, she said, "Right. Now good night."

"Until," he said and jogged off to his car, which he had left running. Teri noticed that he became a little tangled up in his own feet and nearly tripped over the curb.

"Bizarre," she said, shaking her head and closing the door. She made sure it was locked. Then, settling down on her bed-couch in front of the TV, she pulled out the first piece of pizza. But before she could take a bite, the image of the laughing pizza delivery man loomed in front of her, and she couldn't help but chuckle herself. It wasn't as if he were laughing at her. And it wasn't a crazy, haunting guffaw. It was as if this man, who was fast approaching midlife, was so brimming full of joy that it kept oozing out of him in the form of that zany, contagious roar.

Teri bit into the pizza, a broad smile still plastered across her face. And she repeated his little phrase in a fake accent, "Right as right can be!" Then she burst out laughing and realized she hadn't had much cause to even smile today. In a strange way, the laughter comforted her.

Eight

On Sunday morning it rained. Not hard, but a misty sort of rain almost as if God were using a gigantic spray bottle to squirt the inside of this tropical terrarium. The moisture made Teri's long hair coil into a mass of curls. She wished she could somehow pull it back or pin it up. But the volume made it impossible to do anything other than let it run wild across her shoulders and down her back. Nothing short of a machete could tame this jungle of a mane today.

"You about ready to go?" Dan called through the closed bathroom door.

Teri stepped out and said, "I'm ready. Where's Annie?"

"She went back to bed. She's not feeling too terrific."

"Is she all right?"

"I think she will be. On the way home from church remind me to stop to pick up some 7Up and crackers," Dan said.

They drove north toward the Halekuali'i Resort. "Have you been to our church before?"

"No."

"It's different than you might expect. We love it. Not everyone from the mainland feels like we do, though."

"You mean us *haoles* don't fit into your church?"

Dan looked surprised and a little pleased that she had remembered the Hawaiian word. "No, I mean it's not what you're used to. That's all."

When they parked in the church's lot, Teri thought the building looked enchanting. Its appearance welcomed them, with a tall steeple and thick, green foliage around the church's sides. Painted bright white with deep green trim, the structure was one of the original churches built by the missionaries more than a hundred years ago. Dozens of parishioners gathered on the lush carpet of grass surrounding the building.

She noticed several older women standing by the front door dressed in loose fitting, flower print mu'umu'us with fragrant plumeria leis strung over their arms. She guessed they were the official greeters. She also guessed that this church would be quite traditional. Perhaps even some of the service would be given in Hawaiian.

Dan greeted a few of his friends as he and Teri wove their way across the lawn, through pockets of chatting adults and children running around. No one seemed to be in much of a hurry. When they reached the steps, the woman on the right crooned, "Welcome. *Aloha.*" She placed a lei around Teri's neck and softly kissed her on the cheek.

"Thank you," Teri said.

Dan stepped in behind her and gave each of the ladies a peck on the cheek.

Teri entered the church, expecting soft music and pews full of snowy haired women bowed in prayer. Instead people were standing around visiting, while the clear voices of little children singing by the piano at the front greeted her. Then she heard it—the distinct, jovial laugh of the pizza delivery man.

"Hey," Dan said, "Gordon's back! And I can't believe it; he convinced Kai to come to church! Look, over there. Kai's the poolside bartender at Halekuali'i."

Teri glanced at Gordon and then at the bartender. She thought she might have seen Kai at the luau. He had a lei on just like Teri's, evidence that he, too, was a visitor.

"You have to meet Gordon," Dan said.

"We've already met," Teri said cautiously. She looked away before Gordon made eye contact with her and purposefully turned her back to him. It didn't make her feel any better knowing that this crazy man was a friend of Danny's.

"Where did you meet Gordo?"

"Gordo?" Teri repeated. "You actually call him Gordo?" She hadn't noticed him sneaking up behind her.

"Yeah, they actually call me Gordo," he said. "Do you know something I don't know?" His eyes were crinkled shut as he smiled down at Teri. He looked a little different than he had the night he delivered the pizza. Sort of younger. Or cleaner. Or something.

"It's just that *gordo* is a Spanish word," Teri said cautiously. She felt she had been painted into a corner.

"I think I heard that before," he said. "And now, what does *gordo* mean in Spanish?"

Teri looked to Dan for support. He kept silent. "It means 'fat,'" she said in a low voice.

Gordon's laughter bubbled out all over the place. "Well, it

might suit me someday," he said, "but at least not yet." He patted his flat stomach and then extended a hearty handshake to Dan. "Good to see you, Dan. You know Kai, don't you? And Kai, this is Teri."

"I remember you from the other day at the luau," Kai said to Teri. He had a slight grin on his face as if he knew something she didn't.

"Where's Annie?" Gordon asked.

"She wasn't feeling well."

A smile lit up Gordon's face. "Ah, right. Morning sickness."

Teri glared at him. What a cruel joke. How could this guy say something so heartless, especially if he knew what Dan and Anita had gone through trying to have a baby.

"No," Dan said quickly, "we're not pregnant."

"Are you sure?" Gordon had an elf-like quality about his expression. "I've been asking Jesus to touch her womb for quite some time. Wouldn't surprise me if it pleased him to do it now, while her sister's here." His look focused in on Teri. Sincere blue eyes met hers, and he lingered in his gaze.

Teri looked away, and as she did, she noticed Mark coming in the back door. She waved eagerly, motioning for him to join them, which he did. Introductions were made, and Dan suggested they find a place to sit since the pews were filling up. Teri followed her brother-in-law down two rows, and then the four men and Teri all filed in and sat on the hard wooden bench. She wasn't sure how it happened, but she ended up sitting sandwiched between Mark and Gordon. Mark made her feel safe, even in the midst of their unresolved relationship. But sitting next to Gordon, she felt squirmy, as if he had somehow invaded her space.

The children toward the front finished their music practice and scattered to find seats with their parents. Within a few minutes, the narrow church building was packed. Two more people slid into their pew, which meant Gordon scooted even closer to her. She tried to slide closer to Mark without pushing herself against him.

At this moment, Teri hated her thighs. They were large compared to the rest of her body. And sitting down made them spread out, making the seating arrangement even tighter. She glanced down self-consciously and noticed that her thighs were definitely broader than Mark's. Could she ever trust a man who had skinnier thighs than hers? She hadn't felt that way with Scott. Scott was a large man, which made her feel he was just the right size for her. She wished he were sitting next to her this morning instead of Gordon or even Mark.

What was going to become of her relationship with Mark? Teri hoped he would whisk her away after church so they could have a long talk, just the two of them.

A large Hawaiian man in a flowered print shirt strode down the center aisle of the church just then, greeting people as he came. "This is the day the Lord has made," he said in a rich, round voice. "Let us rejoice and be glad in it!"

As soon as he reached the front of the church, the congregation rose to its feet and someone began to play a lively chorus on the piano. Drums and an electric guitar joined in.

Teri hadn't noticed all the instruments before, tucked around on the left side of the church. The sound was invigorating, not too loud, not too jazzy. She liked it.

Then the man at the front started to sing, and the congregation joined in. No words were on an overhead to follow or in songbooks to look at. The singing seemed spontaneous and loud.

It reminded Teri of a little church she had helped to build in a Mexicalli village called Nueva. There the people sang with the same fervor, the same love for God. Putting aside all encumbering thoughts of Mark, Gordon, and Scott and even the size of her legs, Teri closed her eyes and sang out.

After the service they all stood on the lawn, visiting in the cool shade. The fragrance from the creamy plumerias around Teri's neck filled her nostrils and made her smile. She had already told Dan and the others how much she loved their church. Kai was reserved in his comments, saying that church was a new experience for him, but he wanted to come back next week and bring his girlfriend.

Now Teri waited for Mark to say something. All he had to ask was "Teri, do you want to go to lunch?" or "Teri could I talk to you alone for a minute?" Anything to initiate a conversation. But he mentioned nothing. He didn't even look as if he wanted to say anything. Teri couldn't understand how anyone could be so even-keeled, especially when to her they obviously needed to test their relationship to see if anything were there.

Come on, Mark. Don't make me initiate this!

They all walked together to the parking lot. Mark said goodbye, got in his car, and left. Now Teri was mad. How was she supposed to interpret that? If he didn't want to date her, fine. If he didn't want to see her at all while she was here, she could live with that. But this silence was ridiculous. Whatever had clicked between Teri and Mark last summer had definitely disappeared. Poof. Gone. Or at least she thought it was. It was hard to make that final judgment when they hadn't talked one to one.

Teri gave a half-hearted wave to Gordon and Kai. Gordon smiled at her and said his farewell of "Until," and Teri plopped down in the passenger seat of Dan's car. *What is Mark's problem, anyhow? Is there another woman? Fine! Just tell me. Is it me? Did he change his mind since those notes he wrote saying he enjoyed being with me and was looking forward to my coming this summer? What?! I'm going crazy waiting for him to talk to me. As soon as we get home, I'm going to call him. He and I are going to have a heart-to-heart talk and get this settled.*

Feeling fired up enough to make the call right then, Teri was frustrated when Dan stopped at a convenience store on the way home. Dozens of tourists were inside the shop. Teri could spot them easily now. They had a certain frenzied appearance about them, and all their clothes looked new. Dan picked up some 7Up and saltines, and then he wandered off into the pharmaceutical aisle. Teri picked out a few postcards and examined a bin of coconuts by the door. The sign gave instructions on how the coconuts could be mailed to the mainland.

"Ready?" Dan asked, calling to Teri from his spot in line at the checkout. She joined him and looked at the small box he held. It was a home pregnancy test.

Nine

❦

Teri held the telephone receiver to her ear and waited for the answering machine's long beep. "Hi, Mark, this is Teri. It's Sunday afternoon, and I'd appreciate it if you could give me a call. Thanks. Bye."

She was fired up and ready to talk, which made it frustrating to be stuck with an answering machine. Who knew when Mark would check his messages? She hung up the phone and let out a sigh. Dan and Anita were in their bedroom with the door closed. Teri could hear them arguing. She guessed they disagreed about using the home pregnancy test.

Men can be so insensitive sometimes. What do they know about pregnancy? This Gordo-guy suggests this is a good time for Annie to be pregnant so Dan runs out and buys a home test. That's real scientific. Men can be so clueless!

Is that Mark's problem? He doesn't call me or talk to me because he's naturally clueless?

Just then the phone rang and Teri grabbed it, hoping Mark was calling.

"Hey, gorgeous, mind if I pick you up early for dinner tonight? I get off work in about half an hour."

"Scott?" Teri said.

"Yeah, who were you expecting?"

She quickly cleared her thoughts. "You. I was expecting to see you. Tonight."

"So, I can pick you up in an hour, if that's okay."

"Sure. That'll be great! I'll see you. Bye." Teri hung up and ignored her confused feelings about Scott. She wished she were going out to dinner with Mark tonight. She would feel better if she could resolve that relationship before moving on to the next.

To divert her feelings, she concentrated on what she should wear. She still had on the straight skirt and cream colored knit shirt she had worn to church. Was that too dressy? Maybe she should change into jeans. Or shorts. She didn't want to look like a tourist. Yet, if Scott were taking her to some nice place, she didn't want to look too casual either. She settled on the outfit she was wearing convinced, after a few turnarounds in front of the full-length mirror on the hall closet door, that it was flattering and comfortable and best of all, she already had it on.

The argument between Anita and Dan calmed down, and Dan marched into the living room mumbling something to Teri about women being irrational. He plopped in front of the TV and turned on a competition volleyball game.

Teri wondered if she should try to talk to Anita or leave her alone. She finally decided that if she were in Annie's place, she would want her sister to comfort her.

"It's me," Teri said, tapping on the bedroom door and ignoring Dan's glare. "May I come in?"

"Sure," came the calm voice behind the door.

70

Teri went in and sat on the edge of the bed. Anita was curled up under a sheet. Her short hair stuck out, and her eyes looked red from crying.

"You okay?" Teri asked.

Anita nodded but didn't say anything.

"Is there anything I can do?" Teri asked, reaching over and giving her sister an assuring pat on the shoulder. "Do you want anything to eat?"

"No, I'm fine. I don't know what's wrong with me. I wanted you and me to go places and do things together."

"I know. And we will. You need to get over this bug you've caught. We have lots of time."

Anita readjusted her position. "Danny thinks the bug is a baby. Did you know he bought a test?"

Teri nodded. "I was with him."

"I'm not going to take the stupid thing. Do you know how many of these I've taken in my life? Too many! When, or if, I'm ever pregnant again, I'll know."

"Danny was probably trying to help in his own bizarre, masculine way. If it makes any difference, it wasn't his idea. This man at church, Gordo, suggested it. Can you believe people call him, *Gordo?*"

Anita's face lit up. "Danny didn't tell me Gordo was home. How is he?"

"Fine, I guess. He sure is an odd one, isn't he?"

"He's unique, all right. Part maverick, part pioneer, and part saint. He's a fantastic person. Did you know he's a pastor?"

"You can't be serious."

"Really, he is. He's going to school on the mainland. Texas, I think. When he graduates, he wants to come back here and start a church on Maui," Anita said.

"Then why did he come to your door on Friday night delivering pizza?"

"Money is tight for almost everyone who lives here," Anita said. "Gordo is just like the rest of us. He works hard to make a living and trusts God to make up the difference somewhere along the way."

"I can't get used to hearing you call a grown man 'Gordo,'" Teri said. "I actually first met him at the luau. Remember when I told you some jerk spilled Coke on me? It was he."

Anita smiled. "That is his one fault. Gordo is the clumsiest person I've ever met. One time he was helping to serve communion at church, and he stumbled with a tray of bread in one hand and a tray of juice in the other hand. Crumbs and sticky grape juice were on the front pews for months!"

Teri could never picture their father tripping when he served communion. "Was it a total disaster or what?"

Anita started to laugh. "Not with Gordo. He broke into that laugh of his, and the whole congregation busted up. He said his guardian angel must have tripped him because the church geckos weren't getting enough to eat lately."

"Church geckos?"

"You know how people talk about starving church mice? On the islands we have church geckos. They're little green lizards with tiny suction cups on their feet. Gordo said we should leave the spilled communion for them to lick up. It was really funny at the time."

"I guess that's one way to break the mood in the middle of a serious sacrament," Teri said.

"It was actually the best communion I've ever participated in. Certainly the most meaningful. Since Gordo had dumped the bread and juice, he asked if anyone had anything with them that we could use instead. He passed the tray around and collected everything from restaurant-wrapped soda crackers to Life Savers. Someone had half a bottle of orange juice to contribute, and the communion was back on. When he gave thanks and broke the crackers and Life Savers, he talked about how God is a creative, unstoppable God who provides for our needs. He said we should learn to live in the unforced rhythms of grace. I'll never forget it."

Teri checked the clock on the bed stand. "I probably should get ready. Scott called and is coming to pick me up in a few minutes. If Mark phones, tell him I really want to talk to him."

Just then the phone rang, and Anita picked up the extension next to the bed. "You can tell him yourself," she said, handing Teri the phone. "It's Mark."

"Hi."

"Hi," he said. "I received a message that you called."

"Well, I wanted to see if we could get together some time to talk. I know you're busy going out with the whales and everything…"

Anita slapped Teri's leg, and Teri bit her lip. "I don't mean, going out with the whales, I mean going out to sea to see the whales." She rolled her eyes at Anita. This was not going well.

"Actually," Mark said, "the whales are only around during the winter months. I'm putting together all the research information I collected this past winter."

"Well, I'm just saying whenever it's convenient for you, I'd like to get together."

"How about tonight?" Mark said.

"Tonight?" Teri gave Anita a panicked look. Anita shrugged her shoulders and offered no suggestions. "I kind of have something going on tonight. How about tomorrow or Tuesday sometime?"

"As long as it's in the morning."

"Sure," Teri said quickly. "What time? Is ten good?"

"I meant morning," Mark said. "Like six or seven o'clock."

"Oh! Okay. Six or seven o'clock. Should we meet for breakfast somewhere?"

"Do you want to come to Lahaina?" Mark asked.

"I could probably borrow the car," Teri said, looking at Anita, who was holding up nine fingers. "I'd have to be back before nine so Dan could take it to work."

"Then why don't we meet at the Pioneer Inn for breakfast? They open at 6:30."

"Okay, the Pioneer Inn at 6:30. Great! I'll see you tomorrow."

"I'll be looking forward to it," Mark said.

"Now that wasn't so bad, was it?" Anita asked as Teri hung up.

"He said he's looking forward to it. What do you think that means?"

"I think it means you two need to talk, and he's looking forward to it. Too bad you made plans with Scott for this afternoon. Mark has today off. You two could have spent the whole day together instead of a quick breakfast."

"I think it's better this way," Teri said, rising from the bed and checking her reflection in the mirror above the dresser. "I'll see how things go with Scott today and then evaluate it in light of how things go tomorrow morning with Mark."

"If Scott doesn't maul you in the process."

Teri spun around. She was too mad at her sister's comment to respond so she let her fiery eyes speak for her.

"Excuse me for having an opinion of the guy based on our last conversation!"

"Can you just let me be an equal with you, Anita? Just for a few short weeks, let me be an adult, like you, not a naive baby sister who can't make any decisions for herself. Just treat me like a friend. Like a peer. Listen to me, respect me, encourage me. That's all I'm asking. Is that too much?"

Anita looked down at the bed covers and didn't move. When she lifted her eyes, she had a gentler expression. "I can do that."

"I know you can. I need you to."

"Okay."

Teri glanced at the clock again. It had been well over an hour since Scott had called. He should be here any minute. Maybe he stopped by his house first. She could wait. What's a little waiting? She was on Maui time. Time to slow down. Relax. Take it easy.

Teri waited for Scott until 9:30 that night. He didn't come. He didn't call.

At precisely 9:31 Teri heard a knock on the front door. Dan and Anita had gone to bed, and Teri was in her pajamas, an extra-large, yellow T-shirt. She stumbled to the door.

"Forgive me?" Scott asked, holding out a red rose in a white vase. Teri recognized the arrangement as the grocery-store variety.

She didn't know how to respond. All her anger, hurt, and frustration had been used up during the past six hours.

"You could have called," she said in a flat voice that bore neither condemnation nor self-pity.

"The pay phone at the emergency room was out of order."

Teri involuntarily scanned Scott for signs of injury. "What happened?" she asked, her emotions thawing out.

"The nurse said some kids stuck a pog in the phone, and they couldn't get a repairman to come out and fix it."

"Not what happened to the phone! What happened to you?"

"Nothing." A sly smile spread across his lips. "Are you going to invite me in?"

Teri opened the door and with a swooping hand gesture invited him in. His story was bound to be interested.

"Where's Dan and Annie?"

Teri pointed to the closed bedroom door.

"Why don't we go out on the lanai?" Scott suggested.

Teri felt a little uncomfortable wandering around in her night-shirt. But she sat down on the patio chair, folded her arms across her middle, and raised an eyebrow, waiting for his explanation.

"One of the other bellhops pulled his back out on some movie star's trunk. I drove him to the other side, and it took longer than I thought."

"They don't have hospitals on this side of the island?" Teri questioned.

"I'm sure they do, but this guy wanted to go to Wailuku because of his insurance coverage or something. So," Scott said, clapping his hands together, "the night is still young. What do you say we go into town? Are you hungry?"

Teri wasn't ready to forgive and forget. She couldn't spring back instantly, especially when she had plans to meet Mark at 6:30 in the morning. "We can do something another time," she suggested. "It's getting late and—"

"Aw, come on. It's not that late. If you want, we could rent a couple of movies and come back here. I know a great pizza place. We could give them a call, and by the time we picked up some videos, they would be here with the pizza. Sound good?"

"Scott," Teri found it hard to say no to this handsome, blond, tanned man when he sat a few feet away, looking so enthusiastic about being with her. "I don't think it's such a good idea, since Dan and Anita are already asleep."

"Then we can go over to my place. I'm sure Bob wouldn't mind. He's probably not even home. We don't have to make it a double feature. We'll just pick up one video. As a matter of fact, I probably have some lying around the place that we could watch. Kahana Pizza Company will deliver to my front door just as easily as to yours."

Teri thought of Gordo arriving with a pizza at Scott's door with her standing there in her nightshirt. Gordon would probably have a klutz attack and toss the pizza the way he had the communion trays.

"I don't think so, Scott. Let's pick another time and start all over."

He looked like a kid who had just fumbled the winning touchdown.

"Do you want to come over for dinner tomorrow night?" Teri felt responsible to bring things back into a win-win situation.

"I have plans."

"How about Tuesday or Wednesday?"

"I'll call you," Scott said and rose to leave.

Teri felt like saying, "Oh, well, that would be a nice change" but instead said, "Okay. Think about it. Any night this week. I'll make you my award-winning tamales. Old family recipe." She was following Scott to the door and feeling ridiculous that she was attempting to lure him back with food.

Scott turned and smiled. "Tuesday," he said. "I'll be here around seven."

"Okay," Teri echoed the smile. *"Tamales Teresa a las siete a Martes."*

"Teri's tamales at seven on Tuesday," Scott decoded. *"Bueno.*

And don't make me remember any more Spanish than that!"

"I'll see you Tuesday," Teri said as she opened the door for him. "Thanks for the flower."

Scott lingered by the open door, only a few inches from her. He gazed into her eyes and said, "So all is forgiven?"

Teri nodded.

"Bueno." He leaned down as if he were about to kiss her. Instead he whispered, "Tuesday." Then he touched her cheek lightly and left.

Teri felt mesmerized. A swirl of fireworks ignited the instant he bent close to her. She closed the door and slipped back into bed beneath the whirling ceiling fan. Everything was quiet and calm. Everything except the hissing sparklers inside her head.

How did Scott do that to her? Why had she never felt that way with Luis? Teri could tell herself why Scott was not the right guy for her, starting with all of Anita's concerns about his not being serious in his commitment to Christ. If Scott hadn't kept his high school promises to God, why should he keep dinner date promises with Teri?

Still, Scott made her feel emotions she had felt before, but never all together in one relationship. He melted her. And whenever he touched her, there were fireworks.

Now Teri had an even tougher question for herself. Had she really felt those same fireworks with Mark last summer? If so, why had they fizzled out? Was it some sort of enchantment that came with this island paradise? She fell asleep wondering.

The next morning at 6:10, Teri was even more convinced she was in paradise as she drove to Lahaina. The sun had already made its debut over the west Maui mountains and was racing with her down the highway. She passed the Ka'anapali Resort and thought of her first night on the island when they had eaten at Lelani's Restaurant. Mark had told her a whale's skeleton was on display in Whalers Village. They hadn't seen it that night, and now she wondered if he would offer to show it to her another time.

What am I doing? I'm hoping Mark will set up future dates with me. That's crazy! There's nothing between us anymore. Is there? Why is it I go for months—no, years—without any prospective relationships, and now, here I am developing something with Scott and maintaining this unresolved thing with Mark? Weird. Weird, weird, weird.

Teri parked in front of the huge banyan tree and walked over to the Pioneer Inn. For such an early hour, a number of people were out and about. A woman in a weathered straw hat was hosing down the sidewalk in front of the shops behind the Pioneer Inn. She wore a baggy green mu'umu'u, and a stubby cigarette jutted from her lips. Teri guessed this leather-skinned woman had seen plenty over the years here at the Lahaina harbor.

Directly in front of the Pioneer Inn was a dock full of boats of all shapes and sizes. Some of them were filling with passengers already, headed out for all-day sails to neighboring Lana'i and a favorite diving spot, Molokini.

She found the outdoor restaurant at the front of the Pioneer Inn, facing the harbor and the inviting Pacific. Teri had eaten breakfast here with Mark last summer. She remembered his telling her that until the late 1950s this two-story inn was the only visitors' accommodations on that side of the island. It seemed hard to believe that in less than fifty years so much development had taken place in west Maui.

The building looked authentically aged with deep green

walls, red roof, and bright white trim, which might well have been its original colors. She knew Lahaina had been an important whaling port during the mid-1800s. If she had been meeting a man here 150 years ago, he probably would have hunted and skinned whales for a living instead of studying how to preserve them.

"I'm meeting someone," Teri said, as the hostess reached for a menu by the front cash register. She was wearing a mu'umu'u and had her thick black hair wound up in a bun with several white and pink plumerias stuck in the side.

"You want wait or sit?" the young woman asked in the choppy pidgin Teri had heard other locals use last summer.

"I'll sit," Teri said, scanning the few early diners and not finding Mark among them. She was escorted to a booth at the back of the small eating area where she slid onto a thick wooden seat with a high back rest.

"Coffee?"

"Yes, please." Teri looked over the menu while the woman returned with a fresh pot of Kona coffee. Closing her eyes, Teri drew in all the smells and sounds of this morning in Lahaina: the rich aroma of the coffee; the melodic clinking of the ships' bells as they rocked in the harbor; and the mixed chirping and screeching of hundreds of birds who called the banyan tree across the street their home. Another scent drifted her way, the smell of bacon frying in the kitchen right behind her.

Glancing at her watch, Teri decided to order since Mark seemed to be running late. She asked for eggs, bacon, and a short stack of macadamia nut pancakes with coconut syrup. The food arrived before Mark did, and she dove right in. Everything tasted perfect.

She watched a short Japanese man stop along the sidewalk and lean over the wooden railing into the eating area to greet a friend. With no windows, everything was open, warm, and friendly.

A tattered bamboo shade hung over one section of the opening to block the fierce morning sun. Teri remembered Mark telling her last year that *lahaina* meant "cruel sun." Already, at a little past seven, the sun was hot.

Mark finally arrived out of breath and slid into the seat across from her. "I'm sorry. I was hung up on a phone call." He glanced at her breakfast plate. "Did you try their macadamia nut pancakes?"

"Yes, with coconut syrup. They're so good!"

Mark's face softened in one of his close-lipped smiles as he looked at Teri. "Do you remember when we came here for breakfast last summer?"

Teri nodded.

"That was the first time I'd ever tried their mac cakes. I've been hooked ever since. And every time I order them, I think of you."

Teri hadn't expected tender words from Mark. She had thought their meeting would be all cold, hard facts: *The thrill is gone; there's nothing to hold on to; let's just be friends.*

Five minutes earlier she had been thinking about Scott and serving him tamales tomorrow night. How could she switch so quickly and think of Mark? She had to. He was finally sitting down with her. It was just the two of them, and they could talk.

"I wish I had time to eat," Mark said. "I had a message this morning from Claire. Did I tell you about Claire?"

Teri braced herself. This was it, the other woman. This was

why Mark had been aloof since her arrival. Claire.

"Claire is my research partner. She said we have some papers I need to sign this morning so she can fax them today to D.C. It's for an extension on one of our grants. The federal funding people are real sticklers for deadlines. The day's half gone in D.C." He glanced at his watch. "I hate to do this to you. I know you want to talk, and I do too. Can we set up another time?"

Teri felt defeated. It shouldn't be this hard to have a simple conversation. Maybe she was making too much of the whole thing with Mark. Anita could be right. She did tend to analyze the romance out of relationships. It certainly had been analyzed out of this one.

"You know what, Mark," she said. "I don't want this to be a long, drawn out powwow. I was under the impression when I came here that you and I might pick up where we had left off last summer. It doesn't look as if that's what is happening here. So let's not make a big deal about trying to resolve our relationship. Let's both just admit that it didn't work out and get on with our lives. I'll be around. If you have some free time and want to get together, great. If not, that's fine too. Can we just leave it at that?"

Mark maintained his solid-as-a-rock expression. He didn't look relieved or surprised.

"Coffee?" the waitress asked him as she automatically filled Teri's cup.

It took Mark a moment to answer. "No," he said looking up at her. "No thanks. I'm leaving in a minute."

"I'll take the check," Teri said.

The young woman pulled it from her pocket and placed it on the table. *"Mahalo,"* she said and sauntered away.

Teri sipped the hot coffee and looked at Mark. Her mind and heart were flooded with doubts. She wanted to tell him she had been too blunt, too rigid in her approach. She hadn't even given him a chance to say what he thought. Maybe that was because she didn't want to hear it. Better that she reject him before he rejected her.

We're too different, she reasoned. He has his life on the sea with the whales, and I have, well, I don't think I could live on a boat. He's so quiet and reserved. I'm too forceful. I would dominate the relationship…like I am right now.

"Well," Mark said slowly. "I'll do that. I'll call you sometime." Now he looked hurt.

Teri wished she could retract her words and start this encounter over again. She hated it when her sister dominated her, and here she was, dominating Mark.

He slid out of the booth and gave Teri a final grin. *"Aloha,"* he said and strode through the maze of tables and out toward the harbor.

Teri let out a huff and could smell her own coffee breath. Her stomach was in a knot, and she had a painful feeling of remorse. She might never see Mark again. At church perhaps. But she would never know what he really felt. She hadn't given him the opportunity to say anything.

Her emotions wavered all the way back to Dan and Anita's place. She couldn't help but wonder if she had made the right decision.

Dan was waiting for her so he could take the car to work. He seemed especially cheery as he left.

"Annie?" Teri called out as the screen door slammed shut behind her. "Are you up?"

Teri ventured into the bedroom and found her sister sitting up in bed with a peculiar look on her face.

"It's positive," Anita said.

Eleven

Wh, hat are you talking about?" Teri asked, making room for herself on the end of the bed.

"The pregnancy test," Anita continued. "It's positive. I'm pregnant." She still had a dazed look on her face.

"Annie, congratulations!" All of Teri's woes vanished. "Does Danny know? Of course he does. This is fantastic!"

Anita nodded. "Gordo was right, I guess."

"I don't think Gordo had anything to do with it," Teri said. "You're going to have a baby!" She threw her arms around her sister. "No wonder you haven't been feeling well. Do you want me to get you something? Tea or juice or anything?"

"No, it's still too early in the day to think about putting anything in my stomach. I can't believe this. I'm pregnant."

"You don't look too excited."

"I'm scared, Teri. If I lose another baby, my heart will absolutely break."

"Let's pray," Teri said.

"I have been praying."

"I know, but let's pray together. Right now." Teri slid closer and placed her hands on Anita's stomach. Together the two women tearfully asked God to protect the life of this tiny child. When the Moreno sisters were united on anything, there was no stopping them.

"Amen, amen," Teri said. She leaned over, wiped her sister's tears, and in an excited whisper said, "I'm going to be an auntie!"

After their prayer time, Teri decided to spend the day on the beach and give Anita an opportunity to work. By the time Teri returned to the house later that day, she had pretty much convinced herself she had correctly handled the situation with Mark. That relationship was destined not to go anywhere. The fireworks from last summer had fizzled, and there was no rekindling them.

With that relationship settled, she had more freedom to think about Scott. That's how she spent the day at the beach—daydreaming about the tall, blond, handsome dream-come-true.

When Teri had left the house in the morning, Anita was working on several tight deadlines. She was still at the computer when Teri walked in the door.

"Did you finish everything you had to do today?"

"Almost. I called Mom. I told her I was pregnant, and you know what she told me?"

Teri plopped on the bed and slipped off her sandals. "Let me guess. This is our mother, right?"

"Right. The sweet one with the over-protective attitude."

"She probably said you should go to bed and stay there for the next nine months. And you should stop drinking coffee."

"You got it!" Anita said. "Exactly."

"Well, do you think she's right?"

"About the caffeine, of course. All the baby books say that. About staying in bed, I don't think that's very practical or necessary."

"Probably wouldn't hurt to take it easy for the next few months. Didn't you lose the other two at around four months?"

"At three," Anita said.

"So what's wrong with taking it easy for the next three months?"

"Did I ever tell you that you're beginning to sound more like our mother every day?"

"And did I ever tell you," Teri countered, "that you're stubborn as all get out?"

"I'm not going to argue with you, Teri." Anita's face maintained a serene expression. "You're right; I do need to take it easy. I told Mom I would. But you both are acting as if you're the one responsible for this baby. I'm the one who has lost two babies, not you and not Mom."

"Mom lost her first two grandchildren. Did you ever think of that? We all hurt when you did, Annie. You're not alone in this. I'm here for the next few weeks, and I'll only be a phone call away during the rest of your pregnancy." The thought flashed through Teri's mind that Gordon had said it might please the Lord to let Annie be pregnant while Teri was in Hawaii. For the first time she realized what a sensitive comment that had been, especially for a man. Perhaps Gordon was a prophet. He did have the look of someone who had heard heavenly voices.

"I guess the hike through the crater is out for me," Anita said.

"I would think so! I didn't know you were planning on going."

"Danny really wanted me to. I was looking forward to it, but I don't mind sitting this one out. It's a pretty intense hike, from what I've heard. Do you want to go?"

"It might be fun," Teri said, thinking of the good exercise it would be plus the possibility that Scott would go. "Are any spots left?"

"I don't know. It seems to change every day depending on who is able to get time off from work."

"I'd like to do it, but that means you would be home alone. I should stay here with you."

"No, you should go. I'll be fine. This really is a rare opportunity. You can use my backpack and everything. You should go, Teri." Anita pulled back a little and softly added, "I mean, if you want to go. It's up to you."

Teri recognized her sister's effort not to dominate her and smiled in appreciation. "Why don't we wait and talk about it some more when Dan comes home. You want me to make dinner?"

"I can make dinner."

"I know you can. I'm offering to give you a break and do it for you. Or at least help you. Oh, by the way, I invited Scott over for dinner tomorrow night. I told him I'd make tamales."

Anita raised an eyebrow. "Tamales? You're getting ambitious. When do you plan to make them?"

"Tomorrow. Could I borrow the car to go to the store sometime? I plan to make enough tamales to last us the rest of the month."

"Sure, but don't count on me to help," Anita said. "I have too much work to do tomorrow."

"No problem," Teri said, feeling as if she and Annie were finally settling into a more even relationship. "I'm on vacation. I have all the time in the world."

Twelve

❧

Cooking energized Teri, especially a full day in the kitchen, hand-rolling dozens of tamales. It evoked so many wonderful memories. Ever since she was a little girl, the women in her large, extended family would gather on a Saturday three or four weeks before Christmas and spend the day making tamales, hundreds of tamales. They would order pizza to eat while they were working, and she remembered her Aunt Diane would bring an ice chest full of Diet R.C. Cola and drink half of it herself.

At the end of the day, the men would help wash the huge pots and pans, and all the tamales would be divided up between the families and frozen. Teri's family lived off those tamales far into the spring each year.

One of her aunts, Yolanda, was single and didn't particularly like tamales. She used her portion as Christmas gifts each year. When she accepted a new job, her old boss asked if he could pay to remain on the tamale gift list since it had become his family's tradition to eat Yoli's tamales for Christmas Eve dinner.

Anita's small kitchen was much hotter than Mom's had ever been during the December tamale marathons. Teri was sweltering by noon, even with a box fan blowing directly on her. She had a long way to go before she could halt the process.

"Teri," Anita called out, emerging from behind her closed bedroom door, "I'm sorry, but I can't take it much longer. How far along are you? I'm so sensitive to smells right now."

"I'm only about halfway. Do you have another fan around here? Would that help?"

"I'll check with one of my neighbors." Anita left, and Teri wondered how the smell of spiced beef could bother anyone. To her it was one of the wonderful smells of Christmas.

A few minutes later Anita returned, lugging a big box fan.

"Here," Teri said, running to her side, "let me get that. You don't need strain of any kind, remember?"

"My neighbors wanted to know what we were cooking. I told them I'd pay them in tamales tomorrow if I could borrow their fan."

"Good trade," Teri said, taking the fan into the bedroom and plugging it in. "The aroma really is strong in here. I'm glad you have the fan. How's the work coming?"

"It's okay. I wish I could get more motivated about typing all this technical jargon. I feel like a machine. It's not exactly the most challenging job in the world, but it pays."

"And you can stay home with the baby," Teri said. "I think I'd be able to endure a whole lot of boring for the luxury of being with my baby."

Anita looked a little hesitant.

"Are you still nervous about it being okay?"

"Of course. I'm sure I will be until I hold her in my arms and see that she's okay."

"You think it's a girl, huh?"

Anita nodded and patted her flat stomach. "I made an appointment to see the doctor next week. I want to make sure the home test was accurate and that everything is okay, as far as they can tell at this point."

"That has to be the most incredible sensation," Teri said. "To know that you have a tiny life inside you before you can feel it or see it growing. I can't wait until it's my turn. I want at least four kids. Maybe five."

"I recommend you marry first," Anita said with a dry twist of humor in her voice. "First things first, you know. It's always better if their daddy is committed to sticking around for a while. Which reminds me, you haven't said anything about breakfast with Mark. I've been so dazed about the baby I didn't even think to ask you. How did it go?"

Teri bit her lower lip. "Well, I'm not sure. He was in a hurry, and I blurted out that it wasn't coming together for us so we might as well give up."

Anita looked shocked. "You didn't."

"I did."

"What did Mark say?"

"Nothing. *Aloha.* He had to meet his partner, Claire, and sign some papers."

Anita shook her head.

"Don't shake your head at me!"

"I don't understand your logic, Teri. You would give up a man like Mark Hunter just like that," she snapped her fingers for emphasis, "and go to all this trouble of making tamales for a man like Scott Robinson."

Teri didn't want to hear it. "There won't be any tamales if I don't get back in there and finish them. I hope the fan helps." She scooted out, closing the door behind her.

By 5:30, everything was done. The extra tamales were stuffed into Anita's freezer, a dozen or so sat in the refrigerator waiting to be steamed right before Scott arrived, and Teri was debating if she should make the homemade salsa now or take a shower first.

Just then Dan walked in. "Smells good in here. Where's Annie?"

"In there. I overwhelmed her with tamale smells today."

"I think it smells like home. I haven't had a Moreno tamale in more than two years. Annie just doesn't have the time to make them."

"Scott's coming for dinner."

"Scott, really?" Dan paused and said, "Hey, whatever it takes to get you to make tamales is worth it!" He disappeared into the bedroom.

Teri wasn't sure what Dan's opinion of Scott was. She supposed it didn't really matter. What mattered was what she thought of Scott. The best part about his coming tonight was that she felt her relationship with Mark was settled. She could evaluate Scott more accurately now that she wasn't juggling her confusing thoughts of Mark at the same time.

Abandoning the half finished salsa, Teri pulled a clean pair of shorts and a cotton shirt out of the hall closet and headed for the shower. She could finish the salsa even after Scott arrived. Just thinking about the handsome, athletic Scott Robinson coming to see her and eat her tamales made Teri feel good about herself.

Scott was five minutes early, which spared Teri the anxiety of being jilted that she had tried to ward off in the shower. He looked exceptionally good tonight, fresh from the shower with his still-wet blond hair combed straight back and his face clean shaven.

He handed Teri a bouquet of unusual looking flowers. They almost looked plastic.

"They're proteas," Scott explained. "I'm told they grow here. Up country. We'll have to check it out one of these days. I hear an art colony of some sort is up there, too."

"They're unique," Teri said. "Thanks!" She appreciated them more than the grocery-store rose he had brought as his peace offering Sunday night. The rose had drooped and withered before it had even opened its red bud. She found a vase and placed the proteas on the counter.

"Something sure smells good," Scott said.

"I hope you're hungry," Teri said.

The bedroom door opened just then, and Dan and Anita came out.

"How you doing?" Dan said. The two men shook hands. "You don't know what an honored guest you are. The Moreno women don't make these tamales for just anybody, you know!"

Scott reached over the kitchen counter and gave Teri's hand a squeeze. "I'm not just anybody, am I, Teri?"

She was aware of her sister's gaze on them as she answered. "Of course not." She wished she and Scott were alone. Anita's presence was starting to make her feel restricted, and Scott had only been there for three minutes.

"Do you want some help with anything?" Dan asked.

"I thought we would eat outside. Do you want to take these plates and things out for me?"

Dan, Anita, and Scott pitched in, and within five minutes they were sitting down to a mound of steaming tamales.

Dan and Anita, just like Teri, were in the habit of praying before they ate. Scott looked as if he were ready to dig in, when Dan said, "Should we pray first?"

"Sure," Scott said.

"Would you like to pray for us?" Anita asked Scott.

"It's your house. Why don't you pray, Dan?"

Dan prayed. Teri knew her sister had made a note on her mental list: Does not pray. Teri expected to hear about it later and was already making excuses such as, That doesn't mean he doesn't pray at his house. He was just being polite because it's your house.

"Any word on the Haleakala backpack?" Scott asked Dan.

"As a matter of fact, yes. Annie's not going now, so you can take her place if you want."

"They're pregnant," Teri said softly to Scott, as if it were a great secret.

"Congratulations! You want to be, don't you?"

"Yes, of course! Very much so," Anita said. "We've been waiting a long time for this, so I'm going to take it easy the next few months."

"Well, that's great for you, and it's great for me, too!" Scott said. "You're coming, aren't you?" he asked Teri.

She was about to answer "yes" when Dan said, "Well, actually, I gave her spot away. We didn't think you wanted to go, Teri."

"Of course she wants to go," Scott said. "Just tell the other guy you made a mistake, and the place isn't available after all."

"I suppose he'll understand. He's been on this hike before, so

I thought he would be a good unofficial guide for us. But Gordo's pretty easy-going; he'll understand."

"You gave my place to that Gordo guy?" Teri said.

"Yeah." Dan pressed his fork into the steaming, unwrapped tamale and lifted the first bite to his mouth. He closed his eyes and savored the morsel. "Teri," he said swallowing hard, "if you ever want to know how to make a million dollars, all you have to do is sell your tamales. There's nothing like this on the whole island."

Suddenly Scott stopped unwrapping his tamale and locked eyes with Dan. Dan's fork halted midair, steam wafting up from his next bite.

"Are you thinking what I'm thinking?" Scott asked.

A smile edged up Dan's five-o'clock-shadowed jaw. "We could make a million," he said.

CHAPTER

Thirteen

"Okay, wait," Dan said, marking out some numbers on his paper and writing in a new figure. He turned the page so Scott could read it. "If we had the corn husks shipped directly over from the mainland in bulk, we would save a bunch. They're not perishable so we could put them on the slow boat and pay the lowest rate."

"Great idea," Scott said. He drained the last sip of coffee in his cup and leaned back in the patio chair. "The key would be keeping the tamales frozen after they're done."

"We could put a freezer right here. Outside. I could build a shed of some sort to give it shade," Dan said, getting up and marking off the side wall under the kitchen window with his feet.

"You guys will have to excuse me," Anita said, suppressing a yawn. "I'm really wiped out. I'm going to bed. Tell me what you decided in the morning, Teri."

"Okay, good night. Do you guys want some more coffee?"

"Sure," they both said.

Teri followed Anita into the house and in a low voice said, "Annie, thanks for hanging in there. I know it's late. Thanks for being so nice to Scott and everything."

Anita yawned again and nodded her head. "I'll talk to you in the morning, okay?"

"Sweet dreams," Teri called out and then returned to the lanai with the coffee pot.

"The biggest question, I think," said Scott, "is for Teri. Can you make this many tamales? Will you get sick of it?"

"I suppose I would eventually. But I love making them. It's therapy for me. I could teach someone else easily enough."

Dan wrapped his hands around his warm coffee mug. "I'm sure we would have no problem selling them. I think it's an award-winning idea. But it's really up to you. Do you want to start a home business like this?"

"Like I said earlier, I've never given it any thought. Let's pray about it for awhile."

"It would keep you in Maui," Scott said, "and that would be an answer to my prayers." He reached over and grasped Teri's hand. She didn't pull away but surrendered to his touch. They meshed their fingers together.

"It's something to think about," Dan said, standing up and stretching. "I'm going to bed, too. Don't forget to ask for those hike days off, Scott. And remind me to call Gordo tomorrow and tell him the place isn't available."

As soon as Dan left, Scott used his strong grip on Teri's hand to pull her closer to himself. "Hi, beautiful," he said. "I've been thinking about you all day. Do you want to go down to the beach? I found some fireworks left over from the Fourth. I thought we could light up the night sky."

Teri's heart was pounding. Scott didn't have to be a genius to know that the fireworks had begun exploding inside of her the minute he had reached for her hand. "Sure. Let me grab a sweatshirt."

"You don't need to," Scott said. "I'll keep you warm."

She didn't doubt for a minute that he would. Still, it gave her an excuse to stall before they left. Grabbing a sweatshirt from the closet, Teri slipped into the bathroom, closed the door, and scrutinized her reflection in the mirror.

Okay, you big baby. What are you afraid of this time? Why are you turning into this frightened kitten simply because a wonderful man seems to be falling in love with you? Is that it? Are you falling in love with him, Teri? Have you even figured out what love is? Why are you questioning yourself or Scott? Why do you always have to analyze the romance out of everything? Stop it right now! You go to the beach and have a good time with this man. You allow yourself the freedom to fall in love, okay? Okay!

When Teri stepped out, Scott was on the phone. She cleared the dishes as he finished up his conversation saying, "Okay. Tomorrow night. Okay. Yeah. Good-bye."

"Work?" Teri suggested.

"What? Oh, yeah. Work. You ready to go?"

"As soon as I put this salsa in the fridge."

"Did you make this, too?" Scott asked, quickly dipping one more tortilla chip into the salsa before she poured it into a refrigerator container. "You know, we could manufacture this as well as the tortillas."

"I think the price of red chilies is too high here," Teri said.

"Maybe not if we can buy the produce direct from the growers up in Kula. I'll ask the guys in the kitchen at work tomorrow to see what they think."

They drove a short distance up the coast to a remote cove that they had to hike down to. Other cars were parked at the top, and since it was dark and so secluded, Teri couldn't help but feel they were crashing in on a private party. Scott carried a beach towel and a bag full of bottle rockets. They discretely made their way past several couples and found their own private corner of the beach.

Scott spread out the towel and offered Teri a seat. Then he lined up all his fireworks along the shore, securing them in the damp sand. One by one he lit them, and Teri oohed and aahed as the unguided missiles shot into the air. A loud shrill, a brief blast of bright light, and then a whimper came from each rocket as it met its watery grave, twenty or thirty feet out to sea.

"That's it. Not a bad show, huh?" Scott said, joining her on the towel and wrapping his arm around her. "Are you cold?"

"No. It's a beautiful night. Look at that moon."

"I'd rather look at you," Scott said softly in her ear. "Do you have any idea how beautiful you are?" He kissed her neck.

Every impulse within Teri beckoned her to melt into his arms, to surrender to the intense kisses Scott was ready to give her. But in the back of her head like a fire alarm, something wailed, *Stop! Stop! Stop!*

Just as his lips were about to press against hers, Teri heeded the unremitting alarm and pulled away. "Can't we just sit here and snuggle for a bit?"

"Snuggle?"

"Yeah, you know, snuggle."

Teri strained to see Scott's expression in the shadows. She guessed he wasn't too thrilled with the idea. "Then let's walk for a while, okay?" She stood up and offered him her hand.

"You want to walk."

"Come on! We can take off our shoes and play tag with the waves."

Scott rose, good-naturedly asking, "This is the playful side of you, right?"

"It's such a beautiful night. Let's enjoy it. Doesn't a leisurely stroll barefoot on the beach sound romantic to you?" Teri slipped off her sandals and tossed them onto the blanket. Scott did the same.

"What you're really saying is that you want to go in the water. I'm right, aren't I?" He sounded playful as he took the stance of a football player about to rush his opponent.

"No!" Teri squealed, turning to run from him. She knew she was doomed; she couldn't outrun Scott. Her bare feet scrambled through the loose sand, down toward the water where she could at least run faster on the wet, packed sand. She was almost to the water's edge. She could hear Scott thundering right behind her, when she stepped on something sharp and immediately crumbled to the ground.

"Ow!" she cried, grabbing her foot. Scott reached her at that moment and, not aware of her injury, scooped her up and headed for the water.

"Scott," she shrieked, "I'm hurt! My foot!"

He stopped and let her down. In the moonlight reflecting off the water Teri could see a long stick protruding from the ball of her foot. She started to cry as she lowered herself and pulled out the stick of one of Scott's bottle rockets. She could feel the warm blood trickling down her foot.

"What happened?" Scott asked.

"The fireworks," Teri said, trying to catch her breath and mask her tears. "They bit me."

Scott gave a little chuckle at her joke as she handed him the stick. "Are you all right?"

"I think so."

"I better pull the rest of the sticks out of the sand before I step on one. I'm sorry, Teri."

"That's okay. Don't worry about it."

Scott left her for a few minutes, and in that short time the pain escalated in her foot to the point she wanted to scream. Trying hard to control herself, Teri said, "I think part of it broke off inside. It really hurts, Scott."

"Come on, then. Let's get you taken care of." He scooped her up again, this time carrying her back to the towel. "Do you want me to try to pull it out?" he said.

"There's no light here. I think we should go home." The pain was incredible. Teri didn't want to suggest the emergency room, but she was afraid she was seriously injured.

"Do you think you can make it up the trail? I'm not sure I can carry you. It's pretty steep." Scott wrapped his arm around her waist, and she hobbled on one foot through the sand.

The trail seemed insurmountable. She had a sandal on her good foot, which only provided slippery traction on the fine red dirt and sand. More than once Scott caught her before she lost her footing completely. She bit her lip, tried to be brave, and let the silent tears course down her cheeks.

Once they made it to the car, Teri really cried. Scott turned on the dome light and tried to examine her foot. It was covered with blood and sand.

"I think we better try this at home. Does it feel better to keep it elevated?" He wrapped the beach towel around it and settled her foot on the dashboard.

"A little, I guess. I don't know. It really hurts, Scott. It really, really hurts!" Teri let out a wave of tears.

"All right! I know!" he snapped and then repeated more calmly as he started the engine, "I know it hurts. It's going to hurt. I'm taking you home. Don't freak out on me."

"I'm not," Teri said in a small voice. She pulled her tears back inside and tried to control her quivering lips. Scott's patience seemed to have almost reached its limit, and she didn't want to make him angry by letting her feelings gush out.

At home, Scott helped her hobble to the front door and escorted her into the bathroom where he ran warm water in the bathtub. "Put your foot in here," he said, sounding more annoyed than compassionate. "Now let me see what you did."

He pulled her foot up and examined the puncture. "A piece is still in there. Do you want me to pull it out? Where are some tweezers?"

"In that top drawer, I think," Teri said. "How deep is it?" She tried to twist her foot around so she could see. It didn't look good.

"Okay, now hold still," Scott said, arming himself with the tweezers. He grabbed her foot in his strong hand and yanked at the lodged stick.

Teri let out an unbridled shriek, which immediately brought Dan and Anita into the bathroom.

"I'm sorry, I'm sorry," Teri said, feeling numb. The tears started all over again. She felt angry at Scott for being so rough.

Scott explained to Dan and Anita what had happened. Dan suggested they take her to the twenty-four-hour clinic in Lahaina.

"I'll drive her there," Anita said, immediately stepping into her big sister role. "Let me throw some clothes on."

"No, I'll take her," Dan said. "You go back to bed, Annie."

"I can take her," Scott offered.

"No, I'll take her, Scott. You have to be at work earlier tomorrow than I do."

"Well, if you're sure," Scott said.

"I'm sure."

The two men helped Teri out to Dan's car. She felt ridiculous. Yet at the same time, she was in so much pain all she cared about was having the stupid thing out of her foot. Sliding into the front seat, Teri balanced her towel-wrapped foot on the dashboard.

Scott stepped back and let Dan take over.

Fourteen

During the next four days, Teri had lots of time to think. The doctor who had removed the fireworks stick from her foot had left her with eight stitches, a bottle of antibiotics, and strict instructions to stay off her foot for a week. She followed all his instructions and faithfully applied the gel from Annie's aloe vera plant to help the healing. Her grandmother had taught both of them this old remedy.

What Teri thought most about was Scott. He didn't come by on Wednesday, the day after the accident. At first she was miffed. Then she remembered his phone conversation that she had overheard the night before. He had said something about working that night at seven. Yet Dan had said Scott had to be at work early that morning. Teri assumed that he was working a double shift and that he would call her or show up with a bouquet of flowers as soon as he could. But he didn't call or show up.

Teri finally heard from him Thursday evening, when he phoned. He said he had made plans to sail on Friday morning, and he knew she would understand. She did. Sort of. Everyone else's life shouldn't come to a standstill just because hers had.

Annie wasn't the best company. She was struggling with nausea in the mornings and was exhausted if she didn't nap in the afternoons. In between she was furiously pecking at her computer keys, trying to keep up with her deadlines.

Teri camped out on her couch-bed and became well-acquainted with the variety of shows on daytime television. By Friday night she was begging Danny to bring home a video for her—a whole stack of videos.

All Anita wanted was Chinese food, morning, noon, and night. Both Dan and Anita had their restaurant jobs on Friday night, but Danny came home early with Chinese food and six movies.

"You're my hero," Teri said as she popped the last of an egg roll into her mouth. "I'm going crazy doing nothing. I've read three novels, slept until I feel I've rested enough for the next two years, and memorized every commercial on the island." To prove it, she switched into a pirate's voice and recited a slogan from Blackie's Bar.

"Okay, okay, we believe you," Anita said, putting down her chopsticks and heading for the door. "Come on, Danny, I don't want to be late. See you later, Teri. Don't wait up, and don't let any strangers in."

"I won't. You two have a good time, too!"

They left in a flurry, and Teri settled in to watch the first movie. It was a plotless, karate-type movie, and she gave up on it in less than ten minutes. "I should have guessed what kind of movies Dan would rent," she mumbled. "I hope they're not all this cheezy."

She rummaged through the stack and found four macho movies. Then she laughed when she came to *The Sound of Music*. She hadn't watched it since she was a kid, and even then she didn't know if she had seen the whole movie.

Teri popped in the cartridge and settled back as Julie Andrews frolicked in the Austrian Alps, singing her heart out. When Julie Andrews's character, Maria, ran back to the convent, Teri realized she missed walking. And running. And being mobile.

She fell asleep before the movie was over and woke when Dan and Anita came in some time after midnight. She was instantly disappointed. Scott hadn't called or stopped as she had secretly hoped he would.

After Dan and Anita went to bed, Teri lay awake, thinking of how Scott had more or less abandoned her on the night of the accident when he had let Dan take her to the emergency clinic. It seemed odd to her that Scott could drive to the other side of the island to take some guy from work to the hospital two nights earlier, but he could hand her over to Dan without hesitation. Why couldn't he come by to see her when he only lived three blocks away? In the four days since the accident, all he had done was call her once.

Teri phoned Scott early on Saturday morning. But he was already gone, and his answering machine was on. Her message was simple. "It's Teri. Call me sometime."

He finally did on Saturday night. "What a week!" he began. "I've wanted to come by so many times, but it didn't work out. I hope you're all recuperated, because I've made dinner reservations for us."

"Scott, I'm supposed to stay off my foot for a week."

"How long has it been?"

"Four days. Four very long and lonely days."

"And that's exactly why you need to get out of the house. Come on. Don't you have crutches or anything?"

"No."

"Okay, then we'll go to Plan B. I'll bring dinner to you. What sounds good?"

Teri started to relax. Scott was trying to be supportive. "Anything is fine with me. I appreciate this, Scott."

"No problem. Are Dan and Anita home? Should I bring enough for them?"

"That would be great. Annie's into Chinese food lately."

"That's easy. I'll be there in an hour."

Teri hung up the phone and fought the apprehension she was feeling. The last time he had said he would be there in an hour he had arrived almost six hours later. What was it about men like Scott that exempted them from having to operate under the same time constraints and commitments as everyone else?

Teri wasn't sure she liked that. Yet it was part of who Scott was. Maybe she was being too judgmental, like he had said on the sailboat.

Scott arrived within an hour with his arms full of Chinese food, flowers, videos, and a box of chocolate-covered macadamia nuts. It promised to be a fun evening.

And it was. Scott was his charming self, he and Dan conferred about the tamale home business, and even Annie seemed to warm up to him a bit when he handed her a little white box filled with her latest craving, sweet and sour shrimp. Everything seemed normal, like it had last Tuesday night at their tamale dinner. Teri erased her anger toward Scott that had built up during the last four days.

"You'll be back to normal by next Friday, don't you think?" Scott said.

"I hope so. I go to the doctor's on Tuesday."

"Why don't we plan to sail again? Fridays are the best days for me, as long as we're back before noon." Scott had settled into the chair next to the couch. He had on a white T-shirt and deep purple shorts. His hands were folded behind his head, and his blond hair stuck out a little on the sides. He looked comfortable, as if he belonged there, as if he and Teri were already a couple and were going over their plans for the next week. She liked the feeling.

"Hey, Dan," Scott called out to Dan, who was around the corner in the kitchen, "did I tell you I have those days off for the backpack trip?"

"Great!" Dan said, popping his head around the wall. "Teri, I don't think I told you, but another guy dropped out so you and Gordon can both come."

"May I ask a question here?" Teri asked. "Am I the only woman going on this trip?"

Dan looked as if he mentally were going through the list. "I guess you are. You don't mind, do you?"

"I don't know. Are you all planning to turn me into your token female chef and wood gatherer or something?"

"No, it's an equal opportunity bunch of hikers. We'll all pitch in."

"Good, because I'm not interested in being anybody's team mascot."

"You can be my mascot," Scott said playfully.

Teri shot a grimace at him.

Danny returned to the kitchen as Scott said, "Have you ever thought about how differently our lives would have turned out if we had dated in high school?"

She had thought about it, a tiny bit. But she was amazed that thought had entered Scott's mind. "First of all, high school was a long time ago. Besides, I don't think I was your type," Teri said.

"Of course you were. Why do you say that?"

"Well, for one, the culture thing. Not many of you white guys on the football team dated us Hispanic girls."

"White guys? I take offense at that label."

She couldn't tell if he were serious or not. "What do you want to be called?"

Scott thought a minute, and with a smile creeping up his face, he said, "You can call us what the coach called Rick Doyle and me: the Wonder Bread and Miracle Whip Boys."

"I'll remember that," Teri said. "But honestly, don't you think all your traveling has made you more open minded to other cultures? I don't think you would have dated me in high school."

"Sure I would have."

Teri shook her head. "Think back. What girls from a different cultural background did you date?"

Scott seemed to take a long time to reply.

"I know it's a stretch for you, Scott. Admit I'm right. You never would have considered dating me."

"I still disagree, but what's your point? Do you think I have a problem with our cultural differences? I loved your tamales, didn't I?"

"Oh, never mind," Teri said. Their cultural differences had been one of the many concerns she had thought about during her recent invalid days. Dan and Anita seemed well suited to each other because of their similar backgrounds. Teri hadn't thought about the differences that much with Mark since he was so quiet. She actually knew little about his background and heritage. It made her wonder though, if some of the things that seemed normal and acceptable to Scott because of his background would seem unacceptable to her.

Scott's face took on a more serious expression. "Teri, if you're saying you don't think we're compatible because your tan is always going to be darker than mine, I think you're a little 'loco.' I'm very interested in you. Haven't you figured that out yet?"

He had done it again. That soft look in his gray eyes, that low rumbling voice, and his hand now reaching across to grasp Teri's added up to one thing: she was smitten.

"We have good times ahead of us, Teri. Loosen up a little, will you? Let us happen, okay?"

Teri nodded.

By the next Friday, when she and Scott loaded up the *Moonfish* and prepared to set sail out of Maalaea Harbor, she was still feeling smitten by Scott. For six days she had been thinking about this trip. She had seen Scott twice that week, each time for about five minutes when he had stopped by to give Dan a ride to work. She couldn't wait to be up and about again, and this sailing jaunt was her reward for following the doctor's instructions so diligently.

When he had checked her a week after the accident, he was pleased to see how well her foot had healed. She suggested her grandmother's aloe vera as the reason. The doctor had smiled and suggested the expert stitches and miracle of modern antibiotics had cured her.

Feeling as if she had lost an entire week of her precious vacation time, Teri had looked forward to this day of sailing much more than she thought Scott had.

"Okay," Scott called to her from the stern of the vessel, as he motored slowly out of the slip. She was standing on the dock. "Do you remember what you do now? You cast off the bow."

Teri grabbed the rope that held the front of the boat secure and unloosened it quickly. Then holding tight, she walked down the dock until the *Moonfish* was in position to exit the harbor.

"Hop on!" Scott called.

She hopped and landed on her injured foot. A streak of pain shot up her leg. "Ouch!"

"You okay?"

"Yes, I'm okay," she called back, mad at herself for being such a baby.

"Can you grab the buoys, then? Those pads on the sides. They need to be brought in."

Teri went to work, ignoring the twinge of discomfort in her foot and trying her best to remember all the things she needed to do to get the *Moonfish* into full sail once they were out of the harbor. She worked well with Scott, and she worked hard. It took serious arm strength to hoist the sails, and although she wasn't flabby, she wasn't in tip-top shape either.

Teri wondered if she would be able to keep up with the men on the backpack trip. They were leaving in two days, which was not enough time to work on getting into shape.

The sky was clear, and the morning air felt warmer than it had the first time they went sailing. Teri leaned her head back and felt the playful slaps of the wind against her face. She loved the invigorating sensation. No other feeling in the world was like it. The last time they had gone out, Teri had panicked when the wind filled the sails and tipped the boat so far to the side that she thought she would fall out if she let go of her seat. Today she rode with more grace. The sensation made her feel full of life rather than fearful of death.

Teri looked across at Scott. The wind blew his hair in all directions. The smile of an adventurer was hammered across his face like an insignia.

I'm sailing in Maui with Scott Robinson. I can't believe this! This is better than I could have dreamed.

Fifteen

✑

D o you have any idea," Scott whispered into Teri's ear, "how beautiful you are?"

The sailboat bobbed gently on the calm sea. The island of Maui looked miniaturized as they drifted on the sweet blue water, halfway to Lana'i. Teri leaned against Scott's chest and felt his strong, sun-warmed arms wrap around her. He buried his face in her hair and said, "You smell so good. I could get lost in your hair, Julie."

Teri froze. She pulled away and turned to look at him. "Julie?"

"Julie?" he repeated, looking as if he had no idea what she was saying.

"You just called me Julie."

"No I didn't." He smiled and held out his arms for her to come back to him. "I admit it's hard for a man to form his words clearly when his mouth is full of luscious hair. But you didn't hear me correctly." Scott shook his head, retaining his innocent look. "Julie?" he repeated with raised eyebrows. "Where do you come up with this stuff?"

Teri scrutinized his expression and decided he was either a very good liar or was telling the truth. Nothing in his cool demeanor hinted that he had slipped up.

"You know," Scott said, drawing himself up to a seated position, "this is what we keep having problems with, isn't it? You're too uptight."

"No, I'm not."

"Well, it would sure help me if you could figure out what your problem is. It's like you don't want us to happen."

"That's not it, Scott."

"Then what's the problem?" His voice was loud and commanding like it had been in his car the night she had stepped on the fireworks. Her tears had angered him that night. She refused to cry now.

"I'm a cautious person," Teri said, trying to sound strong and confident. "You don't have a problem with that, do you?" Scott ran his fingers through his hair and didn't answer.

Teri felt awful. The romantic mood was broken. Even though Scott seemed to be controlling his anger, she could tell he was mad at her. She sensed he was a smoldering volcano inside.

"Let's head back," Scott said firmly. He pushed himself up and went about his tasks with the sails as if he were a robot.

"I'm sorry," Teri said.

He smiled back his thin acceptance of her apology.

She wanted him to come back to her and hold her and assure her that she was the woman he adored. The tension was awful. How could everything be so good and turn so terrible in a few short minutes?

Teri was convinced it was she. Scott was right; she was too

judgmental, too rigid. Even in the middle of a wonderful, intimate moment, she was so untrusting she was actually hearing things.

That's it! I'm changing. From this moment on, I'm going to be open, free, and trusting. The next time Scott takes me in his arms and kisses me, I'm going to kiss him right back, and good! I'll show him I'm not an uptight prude. If I let this man get away from me, I don't know what I'll do. Another man like Scott Robinson will never be in my life again!

As convinced as Teri was of her course of action, her whole self had a hard time entering into the plan. She was raised to be modest and careful of how she used her body and her actions. It would take a little while for all the parts of her psyche to act on her decision.

Their sail back to Maalaea Harbor was silent and tense. Ignoring the problem between them, Scott talked about work on the drive home. He seemed to be comfortable and acted normal with her, as if nothing unsettling had happened an hour earlier. Maybe it hadn't been as unsettling to him as it had been to her.

"Do you want to come to church with me on Sunday?" Teri ventured during a lull in the conversation. "You said you wanted to start going back to church."

Scott looked straight ahead, waiting for the light to change. They were in Lahaina, right next to the huge, black smokestack of the sugar cane refinery. "Not this Sunday. Maybe next week."

"What's your work schedule like?" Teri took another stab. "Would you like to do something tomorrow or Sunday afternoon?"

"I'll have to give you a call." The light turned green, and they made their way through the late morning congestion and headed north toward Napili.

"I'd really like to get together and do something, if it works out for you," Teri said. Then, draping her arm over the back of his seat, she started to rub his neck.

Scott cringed at her touch. "Sunburn," he said.

She quickly pulled away her arm. "Oh, I'm sorry."

"Why do you do that?"

"Do what?"

"Say you're sorry all the time. It's not your fault my neck is sunburned. You don't have to apologize for trying to do something nice for me like rubbing my neck. Actually, I'm glad you're loosening up a little. I like it when you make a move toward me instead of my always making the moves toward you."

Teri kept that in mind. The minute they pulled in front of the house and Scott turned off the ignition, she leaned over and kissed him on the cheek.

"Thanks for taking me out," she said, looking into his eyes. "I loved being with you, and I'm already looking forward to the next time."

Scott looked pleased, as if this were the kind of treatment he had been waiting for. He sat there, soaking it up.

"You're right about my being too rigid," Teri said, trying to make her brown eyes as expressive as they could be. "I'm going to work on that. You'll see." Then she tilted her chin up and invited him to kiss her.

It was a mutual kiss, one she willingly gave and one he willingly took. In this new balance, Teri felt a sense of power. Neither of them could deny the fireworks between them.

"That's more like it," Scott said, burrowing his nose in her hair. "I knew you must feel something for me. Why haven't you kissed me like that before?"

"I need to go slowly, Scott. Very slowly. Do you understand what I'm saying?"

"Of course I understand. Why didn't you say so? The way you've been pushing me away, I thought I repulsed you or something."

Teri pulled away and looked at him, shocked. "How could you think that? Of course not, Scott. I'm very attracted to you. I'm sorry I made you feel I wasn't."

He lifted his finger and touched her lips the instant she said the word "sorry."

"Oh, I did it again, didn't I? I'll work on it."

"Good," Scott said, straightening up. "I wish I didn't have to go to work. I'll call you when I get off."

"Okay," Teri whispered back. "Bye, Scott." She pulled away and let herself out of the car.

He waved. She waved. Her heart was still pounding. Teri smiled all the way to the front door. As Teri opened the screen door, her sister was standing there with her hands on her hips.

"Hi," Teri said cheerfully, walking past her and heading for the refrigerator for something to drink.

Anita followed her. Holding up both her hands, Anita looked at the floor and said, "I know you don't want to hear this."

"Hear what?" Teri popped the lid on a can of soda and skimmed past Anita on her way to the couch.

"I saw you and Scott in the car just now, and it concerned me."

"Why? There's nothing to be concerned about."

"Teri, I want to know what's going on with you and Scott."

"Nothing is going on. We went sailing. We've spent some

time together. We like each other."

"It looks as if you're getting very involved with each other. Do you really think that's a good idea, Teri? He's not the right man for you. Why can't you see that?"

"Hey, I don't know if he is the right one or the wrong one, but I have the right to figure that out on my own, don't I? How many times do we have to go over this? You are not my mother. Okay? Repeat this after me, 'I am not Teri's mother.'"

"But I am Teri's sister, and as such I'm telling you Scott Robinson is not the right man for you."

"Oh, and you have this on good authority, do you? You know these things? What are you saying, Anita? That God talks to you, and he doesn't talk to me?"

"Maybe so."

"You're crazy."

"Am I? Then answer one question for me. Have you really prayed about Scott and asked God to show you what his best is? I know you've watched lots of movies since you've been here and read a couple of novels, but I haven't seen you read your Bible. You used to be the one who never missed her quiet time when we were growing up. What's happened to you, Teri?"

Teri could feel the anger bubbling up within her. "I'm not into your guilt game, Anita. You're not my mother, and you're not the Holy Spirit. Do you want me asking you when your last quiet time was? Or do you want me accusing you of not trusting God about your baby? You're so quick to judge everyone else. You're not perfect! Just leave me alone. Okay?" Teri jumped up and marched to the front door. "I wish I'd never come here!"

She slammed the screen door and began to march down to the beach. In all the years and in all the arguments she and Anita had had, this was the worst. Never before had she wanted to hit her sister, which is how she felt right now.

Teri broke into a jog and ran almost four blocks before she felt her sandal rubbing the scar tissue on her foot and sending shooting pains up her leg. She took the rest of the journey at a slower, more deliberate pace, blazing a trail down to the beach and heading for some black lava rocks that jutted into the water. She could see someone coming from the other direction who seemed to be headed to the same spot.

Don't you dare think of going there! That's my spot. I found it first!

Teri quickened her pace and scrambled up the low side of the rock, ignoring the other person. She stood on top, pushing herself to her full height, proving to any and all onlookers that she had staked a claim to this spot. Surely that other tourist would keep on walking. Nobody in his right mind would want to deal with Teri in the emotional state she was in at this moment.

"G'day, Teri," came Gordon's cheery voice behind her. "Imagine this! You've come to my favorite prayer closet."

Teri spun around and gave Gordon a glare that would frighten even a pirate. But she never knew if he saw her glare or not, for at that precise second, Gordon slipped on the wet rock. In an effort to steady himself, he lunged for Teri's arm. She tried to pull away. It was too late. In one ungraceful tumble, both of them catapulted off the rock and fell into the water.

Sixteen

❧

Teri came up gasping for air and spitting salt water. Gordon bobbed up a moment later, laughing and choking and laughing some more.

"It's not funny!" Teri croaked at him just as a wave swept over her and tumbled her closer to shore. She half crawled and swam the rest of the way, with Gordon right behind her. Several people on shore had seen the accident and rushed over to check on them.

"Are you okay?" a plump woman asked. "Is there anything I can do?"

"No," Teri said, pushing her hair off her face. She panted for another breath. "I'm fine."

"No harm done then?" Gordon asked, standing up and wringing out the tail of his Hawaiian print shirt.

Teri repeated her menacing glare at him, only this time her fury was waterlogged.

The gawkers dispersed. Gordon smoothed back his thick brown hair. His eyes were still crinkled up, and he was smiling, but he wasn't laughing anymore. He knelt down in the sand next to Teri and looked tenderly at her. She had never noticed his dimples before. They gave him a little kid look. His eyes, fully opened and looking deeply into hers, were as blue as the Maui sky that formed a backdrop behind his head. Gordon's hand gently rested on her shoulder. "Are you sure you're all right, Teri?"

She kept looking at him. Nothing inside her said, *Pull away;* nothing made her feel afraid of this man. Perhaps knowing he was a pastor, or at least planning to be one, made her feel fearless around him. All she knew was that he had a mysteriously calming effect on her.

"Yes, I'm okay."

"Yes, well, right then." He removed his hand and sat down next to her. She faced the shore, and he faced her. "Being that you're all right, then I've a favor to ask of you."

"A favor?"

"You see, I'm going back to seminary in the fall. I know they're going to ask me for a report, and it might help the status of my graduation, you see."

Teri couldn't imagine what he was talking about.

"It regards my duties as a pastor. So, if you don't mind answering honestly, for the seminary report and all, would you rate this baptism a successful one?"

A slow laugh pushed its way up from somewhere deep inside Teri, and she laughed like she hadn't laughed in days, maybe weeks.

"I'll register your response," he said. Then standing up and pulling off his shirt and soggy tennis shoes, he hitched up his swim trunks and said, "A little swim sounds good right about now, don't you think?"

Teri couldn't refuse. She still had on her bathing suit from the sailing trip that morning, and everything else was already wet. Why shouldn't she agree to plunge back in the water with this man? She slipped off her sandals.

He flashed her a smile and headed for the water. Teri peeled off her wet shirt and shorts and watched him dive in.

Slowly strolling to the water, she realized how warm the ocean felt. The splash from the rock had felt refreshing. She had only been in the water two or three times during her vacation, and she considered that a crime. She loved the water. She loved swimming. A relaxing swim would help her mellow out a little and prepare her to face her sister.

She stood at the water's edge, wedging her feet into the warm, wet sand and watched Gordon dive like a dolphin under the next wave. It crested over his submerged body and raced to shore, where it swirled around Teri's ankles and used every one of its tickling, foaming fingers to coax Teri into the water. Chasing the wave back out to sea, Teri dove in and swam out to Gordon.

"Have you ever seen a more beautiful day?" Gordon asked. He tilted his head toward the seamless blue sky and, at the top of his voice, shouted, "Good job, God! You made a winner!"

Teri thought Gordon had to be the most peculiar, free-spirited person she had ever met. Something drew her to him. She couldn't even begin to guess why. He was a klutz. He had dumped her into the ocean. He was from a different culture, and although she wasn't sure of his age, she would guess he was from a different decade as well.

As they bobbed about on the waves, Teri decided she must be drawn to him because of his pastor-side. When she was near him, she felt a strange mixture of joy and peace, two elements that had not been present this morning on the sailboat with Scott. What was it Anita had said about Gordon's sermon after the fumbled communion? Something about the unforced rhythm of grace. Teri longed to feel that way.

For a moment, she considered confiding in Gordon and asking his advice on Scott. But something told her that he too would urge her to break it off with Scott before she was hurt.

They rode a couple of waves to shore, then swam back out to tread water and wait for the larger swells to come in. They didn't talk much, and yet Teri didn't feel uncomfortable. In every way she felt free, free to be herself, free to say and do whatever she wanted.

She only felt a little uncomfortable about her thighs when she and Gordon left the water. But her discomfort was minimal compared to how she felt around Mark or even Scott. Gordon seemed to view everything on such a spiritual plane that he didn't notice less important aspects like physical appearances. He reminded her of her father in that way.

Teri wished she had a towel. Her clothes were already dry, baked nice and warm. She shook out the sand and used her stiff shirt to wipe off her face.

Gordon shook his hair out at the water's edge. He reminded her of some of the guys she knew in high school who surfed. They had a certain look, a certain build. Gordon looked like a vintage surfer.

"By any chance do you surf?" Teri asked when he joined her.

"How did you know?"

Teri shrugged. "You seemed to like the water."

"Some of my mates and I made it into the finals in Australia."

"Really? When was that?"

"Let's see, oh, round eighteen years ago."

Teri laughed. "I was in kindergarten."

"Then I don't suppose you had much interest in watching the finals on the tellie that year. I blew out my eardrum on national television. This one." He pointed to his right ear. "The board caught the underside of a wave and curled up like this." He used his hands to demonstrate. "It flipped out the side and came down on me, like a hammer pounding a nail through a piece of paper."

"Did you lose your hearing in that ear?"

"What?"

"I said, did you—" She noticed his smile and realized he was joking.

"I can pick up some loud and shrill sounds. But for the most part it's gone. Played havoc on my equilibrium. Your turn."

"My turn for what?"

"What's your best lifetime accident?"

"Well, I stepped on a stick from a bottle rocket last week." She showed him the tender spot on her foot.

Gordon made a face, expressing his pity. It looked kind of silly.

"Okay, so it's not a lifetime handicap. You win."

"I have more."

"What?" Teri said. "More handicaps you want to share with me?"

"I don't want to share them with you. I just want to tell you about them."

"Why?" Teri felt like laughing.

Gordon turned serious and thought a minute before saying, "I think you need to know."

Teri suppressed her laugh. She had never met anyone who spent his first conversation with her showing off injuries.

"See this gold tooth back here?" He tipped his head back and opened his mouth, revealing a gold cap on his top right molar. "Got that after I tried to open a beer bottle with my teeth."

"That's a joke, right?"

"No. Did that two years after the surfing accident. And see this?" He showed her a thick scar that ran down the outside of his little finger, all the way to his wrist. "Got that in a motorcycle accident when I was fifteen."

"Any more?" Teri asked teasingly when he had finished.

"That's it. And they're all on the right side. The left side of me is in pretty good shape. Do you like coffee?"

Teri blinked at his illogical question. "Yes."

"Good."

Then they were silent. Gordon looked out at the ocean, deep in thought. Teri felt sure he was going to ask her out for coffee. Why else would he have asked if she liked it?

"I became a new creation in Christ eight years ago."

Teri had never heard anyone phrase it quite that way. But then, with Gordon's obviously wild past, perhaps the most important thing to him was that he did start over fresh when he became a Christian.

"And you?" he asked.

"I think I was three. Maybe four. I prayed with my mom in my bedroom one night and gave my heart to Jesus. You know my dad's a pastor, don't you?"

Gordon nodded. "You don't bite your nails, do you?"

"Not usually," she said, her patience beginning to stretch. "Why do you want to know?"

"That's about the only thing I can't tolerate. That and Halloween."

"Well, good," Teri said, looking him over. "It's good to know those kinds of things about a person, I guess."

"What don't you like?" Gordon asked, his steady gaze resting on her.

"I don't know. Soap operas on afternoon television, I guess. And arguing with my sister, which I did this afternoon. I need to get back and make amends."

Gordon kept looking at her as if he were trying to read her thoughts, like he had the night he had dropped off the pizza. Now he was holding her with his gaze. Teri almost felt he was embracing her without moving a muscle. She should have felt uncomfortable, but she didn't.

"I better go," Teri said, standing and putting on her shorts.

Gordon rose too. "I'll look forward to our next divine appointment," he said. "What was this one? The third?"

"Is that what they've been? Coke on my leg, pizza delivery, and a near drowning—all divine appointments, huh?" Teri shook out her shirt and slipped her arms into the sleeveless holes. "Maybe your guardian angel and my guardian angel should do lunch sometime. That way they can each check their books and make sure we don't have car collisions or capsized boats on our divine appointment calendars."

Gordon smiled broadly.

Seventeen

Anita helped Teri adjust the strap on her backpack and gave her advice on the best level for the waist band to ride. The two sisters had made peace Friday afternoon when Teri returned from the beach, completely exhausted and thoroughly humbled.

She hadn't seen Scott all weekend, which had given her more time to think and to take her sister's advice to pray. Teri had also returned to a regular routine of reading her Bible, a habit that hadn't carried over to her vacation schedule.

Now it was Sunday evening. In the morning Teri would leave with Dan and the ten other men for the "once in a lifetime" backpacking experience.

"Dan says they have wool blankets and pillows in the cabins so I only gave you a sheet and a pillow case," Annie said. "I also put the rain poncho in this top section, here." She pulled out a small, flat, gray plastic pouch with a snap closure. "It's tiny but efficient."

"Do you really think we'll have rain? It's been perfect the

whole time I've been here, except for that one drizzle a few Sundays ago."

"Believe me, it's a whole different world on the other side of the island. Remember when we went to Hana last year? This is the dry side of the island. You're hiking down into a tropical rain forest."

"Okay, okay, I believe you. Thanks for letting me use all your stuff."

"I'm glad you're going."

"I think I'm glad I'm going, too." Teri took off the backpack and leaned it against the wall. She wanted to sit down with Anita and have a heart-to-heart talk, but something inside her wouldn't allow her to open up. She hadn't told Annie about meeting Gordon at the beach on Friday, and she had acted all weekend as if it didn't matter that Scott hadn't called as he said he would.

Teri didn't think she was ready to spend the next few days in close quarters with both these men. At the same time, she wasn't ready to forfeit this camping trip because of the tension she felt.

And the tension wasn't just with Scott. Now she felt uncomfortable thinking about being around Gordon. It was ridiculous for her to feel that way, and she knew it. It couldn't be a romantic thing. They were too opposite. But now she found herself strangely drawn to him.

When she had seen him at church that morning, she had wished he would sit by her as he had two weeks earlier. He had greeted her, and his smile and handshake had been warm and friendly. But he had Kai and Kai's girlfriend with him. Gordon sat with them across the aisle.

During the service, right after the singing, the "keiki choir" was announced. All the children scooted up to the front and sang a sweet song. The first two verses were in English, the third in Hawaiian. As they scattered back to their seats and their parents, the pastor recited a verse about children being a blessing from the Lord.

Teri could feel Gordon looking at her across the aisle. She turned her head just slightly to meet his gaze. He smiled at her and gave a wink that was so slight she wondered if he had a twitch in his eye. She turned her attention back to the front and tried to remember which eye it was. It was the right. That explained it. Hadn't he admitted that his whole right side was short-circuited?

If it was a wink, I'm sure he meant it for Annie since he probably feels proud of himself for predicting her pregnancy.

Instead of talking with Annie this evening, Teri settled for an early night to bed. She and Dan were planning to leave at 6:30 the next morning to meet the rest of the group up at the top of the mountain.

She found it hard to fall asleep with so many unresolved situations in her life. Trying to avoid dwelling on her men problems, Teri started to turn the job situation around in her mind. Part of her wanted to stay on Maui, another part wasn't ready to give up the easy, predictable life she led in Glenbrooke. Life didn't seem to be normal here for her.

Dan kept talking about the tamale idea. He was convinced that if they could find the start-up money, Teri could produce tamales four days a week, six hours a day, and they could make more money than he was making now at the resort.

She wasn't opposed to the tamale idea. It was a good idea. But how many tamales can one person make without going crazy? Still, it could be done. Other people had built financial empires on nothing more than hard work and a good cookie recipe. Dan had checked out some books from the library and was studying all the angles.

If she stayed on Maui, how long could she live with Dan and Anita? And where would her relationship with Scott lead? He sounded ready to make a commitment when they were together. Then he would go days without seeing her or without calling her. She knew he had long hours. So did Dan. But Dan worked a second job, and Teri still saw him more than she saw Scott. She fell asleep contemplating her relationship with Scott.

She found herself still thinking about it the next morning as she and Dan drove along Highway 30 toward the volcanic mountain, Haleakala. Teri was ready for another opinion and her brother-in-law seemed like a good choice. "Do you think I'm interested in Scott because I never had a boyfriend in high school?"

"I don't know. Do you?"

"I've certainly thought about the possibility more than once."

"Do you love him?"

"I don't know." Teri felt depressed that she couldn't answer that question with any conviction. She didn't think she had ever really been in love with anyone. With Luis, of course, she had experienced a certain level of love. But her feelings were not true enough or deep enough to last.

What did she really feel for Scott? She experienced a whole basketful of feelings when she thought about him, including fireworks. That was important.

"Annie doesn't think he's the right one for you."

"I know that."

"But I wouldn't be surprised if she's a little jealous of you."

"Jealous? Why?"

"Because you're the little sister, and you're dating the star from her class while she is stuck with me."

"Annie is *not* stuck with you. She's crazy about you! You guys are going to have a baby. Why would she be jealous of me?"

"You have your freedom," Dan said. "You're still going out and having fun. A lot of options still are available to you. Her life is pretty well figured. That's why I think this tamale business would work. It would give her something new to do. She's been working at the same job for more than six years."

"Nothing wrong with that," Teri said.

"You know Annie; she likes variety. Adventure. It's killing her that she can't come on this trip. As much as we both love living here, she is the one who gets island fever the most."

"I didn't know any of this," Teri said. "Why doesn't she tell me these things?"

"Why don't you tell her the things that you struggle with?"

He had her there. Teri had held back from her sister ever since her vacation had begun. Why did she think they were close?

"I'll tell you why," Dan said. "Because you both spent the majority of your lives in the fish bowl of being the pastor's kids. I think it's obvious, but Annie doesn't see it. You both became conditioned to live in a way acceptable to the people who were watching you. Now nobody's watching, but you haven't figured out who the real you is. So when you hurt, instinct kicks in, and you hide where nobody can see your mistakes."

"That's pretty intense psychology there, Dr. Dan."

He shrugged his shoulders and in an exaggerated German accent said, "I have been observing my patient for many, many years now. I believe she will need quite a few more years under my care before she is completely cured."

Teri punched Dan's arm. She admired him. Annie didn't know what a prize her husband was. He understood her completely and loved her unconditionally.

That's what Teri wanted. If truth be told, she was the jealous one, jealous that Annie had such an incredible person to share her life with.

The sun was climbing through the clear morning sky as they turned up Highway 37 and headed toward the cloud-wreathed volcano.

"It's so beautiful," Teri murmured.

The road led them through Maui's quiet upcountry. The lush green of the foothills and the abundance of colorful flowers reminded Teri of the Willamette Valley of Oregon.

"It's so different from the beach. Do you guys come up here often? If I had island fever, I'd come up here for a few days."

"Unfortunately, no. We've only been here a dozen or so times. With work and everything it's hard to get away."

They passed a few rickety looking mailboxes clumped together at the end of a tree-lined lane. "Do many people live up here?" Teri asked.

"Sure, lots of people. I have some friends up in Ulupalakua who are *paniolos*. I went to the rodeo with them last year in Makawao."

"And I'm supposed to know what you're talking about?"

"They're cowboys. Actually, *paniolo*s is Hawaiian for *Espanoles.*"

"Cowboys from Spain?"

"California. One of the Hawaiian kings, Kam III, I think, brought three Spanish-Mexican cowboys over from California about 150 years ago to raise cattle. Some of the *paniolos* who work at Ulupalakua today are descendants of those three originals."

"That's quite a story," Teri said.

"It's true. It's a whole different Maui up here."

"Sounds like it," Teri answered, gazing out the window at the breathtaking countryside as it rolled past her. She was only half-listening to Dan. Something had clicked inside her when he had mentioned the Hispanic cowboys from California. She realized that since she had been here, she had seen the widest variety of cultural background she had seen anywhere.

In her small Oregon town, she was one of a handful of Hispanic residents. It had never been a problem, and she never had felt discriminated against. But always present in her mind was the underlying truth that she was different from the majority of the people in her community.

On Maui, however, the population was such a melting pot that she didn't stick out. At least she didn't feel as if she stuck out. If anything, she blended in with the natives because of her skin tone. It was one more reason she should consider moving to Maui.

Eighteen

❧

I s this the top?" Teri asked as Dan turned down a road marked by a sign that said "Hosmer Grove."

"No, we're only about seven thousand feet up. The top is more than ten thousand feet. This is where we're meeting the rest of the group. The trail begins up the road from here."

"I can't imagine that winding road going much farther up."

"Oh, it does." Dan parked the car and looked out the windshield to see if any of the guys gathered around the picnic table were from their group. "It's the only road in the world the goes from sea level to ten thousand feet in forty miles. Do you feel a little dizzy?"

"No."

"Some people do. It's an intense altitude adjustment. And it's a lot colder up here. I've been to the top once when there was snow."

"Snow? On Maui?"

Dan opened his door and called back to her, "You can even ski on the Big Island when it snows."

Teri pulled on her sweatshirt and joined Dan outside. It was chilly. She spotted Scott over at the picnic tables with Kai, Gordon, and a bunch of men she didn't know.

Scott left them immediately and jogged over to her. He gave her a tender kiss on the cheek in full view of everyone and then tangled his fingers in her hair. "I've missed you."

"I've missed you, too," Teri said. She found it easy to forgive him. After feeling angry and frustrated at him for not calling, all it took was one soft phrase and one tender touch, and she was putty.

With Scott's arm around her and his fingers still playing with her curls, the two of them walked over to the group. Teri could feel Gordon's smile on her before she actually looked at him. He watched every step she took and kept looking at her after she sat down on the top of the picnic table.

Spread out beside her were bags of food and other camping supplies. The men were talking about how they planned to divide it all up between the twelve backpacks.

"I think those of us with the bigger packs can handle most of it," one of the men said. "And if any stuff is left over, you guys and Julie can take it."

"This is Teri, not Julie," Dan said. "I guess you all don't know her. Annie's sister, Teri."

The man glanced at Scott and then back at Teri. "Teri," he repeated. "My mistake. Nice to meet you. I'm Ron."

The rest of the men introduced themselves in turn, and she tried to appear calm and casual. The coincidence was too obvious to ignore. First Scott called her Julie on the sailboat, and now some guy who sees Scott with her assumes her name is Julie.

As soon as the backpacks were loaded, Teri pulled Scott off to the side under a grove of tall cedar and pine trees. "Who's Julie?"

"Beats me," he said. "Julie, Teri. The names sound pretty similar. I can see why he was mixed up."

"And why did you get mixed up on the sailboat?"

"I didn't get mixed up. Didn't we already go over this?" Scott looked down at the ground and shook his head. It was almost a gesture of pity. "I thought you were going to work on this paranoia thing. When are you going to ease up and start trusting me?"

Teri felt ashamed.

"I'm sorry," she said.

Scott cupped her chin in his hand and tilted her face up toward him. "No more 'I'm sorry's,' remember?"

Teri nodded.

Scott looked as if he were about to say something, but he was interrupted by a Frisbee that sailed inches past their heads.

"Whoa! Sorry there!" Gordon came jogging over to retrieve the Frisbee.

Teri pulled away and felt her cheeks warming. "Is everyone else ready?" She needed to talk with Scott but not here, not like this.

"Looks like it," Gordon said. "No hurry, though. We have all day to get there."

"Dan said you've been on this hike before, Gordon," Teri said.

"That's right. Quite a few years back. We hiked out through Kaupo Gap and down to the ocean. Can't go that way any more. We have to hike out the way we go in." Gordon began walking back to the picnic tables.

Teri followed him with Scott beside her, his arm around her shoulder.

"Can you smell them?" Gordon asked.

"What, Dan and the boys are smelling bad already?" Scott joked.

Gordon ignored Scott, caught Teri's eye, and drew in a deep breath. She did the same. "It's the eucalyptus trees. I haven't smelled them since I left home."

Gordon drew in another breath of the strong eucalyptus. Teri glanced at Scott as he rolled his eyes. "I like it, too," Teri said, suddenly feeling she needed to come to Gordon's defense. "We had eucalyptus trees in Escondido. Do you remember those gigantic ones at the back of the school, Scott?"

Scott looked at her as if to communicate that the last thing he would remember about high school was a tree.

"You two went to high school together?" Gordon asked.

"Sort of. Same school, different years." Teri didn't feel she had to explain anything to Gordon, but she wanted to.

They all hoisted their backpacks over their shoulders, tugged up their socks, laced their hiking boots, and started on their way. Teri had borrowed Annie's boots, which fit a little loose. She was wearing two pairs of socks, and they seemed to feel just right.

They hiked along the side of the winding road, single file, until they reached the trail head of the Halemauu Trail. The minute the crater came into full view, Teri stopped and caught her breath. She hadn't expected all the colors. Thick clouds hung over the higher pinnacles farther up the road. But where the group entered the crater, the sun shone and an eerie wind blew up at them.

"There's no place like it on earth," Gordon said to Teri and two other hikers who had stopped to catch their breath. He took a swig from his water bottle. "Wait until we get inside. You'll think you're on the moon."

"By any chance, does anyone know the last time when this guy erupted?" Teri asked, gazing down into the deep crevices.

"Late seventeen hundreds, I think," Gordon said.

"That doesn't mean he's thinking of blowing off a little steam any time soon, does it?"

"No, safe as a kitten. They monitor all activity at Science City up at the top. I had a friend who worked there," Gordon said. "I went up the night Haley's Comet whizzed by. Had a good look through his telescope. One of the thrills of my life."

"Doesn't take much to entertain you, does it, Gordo?" Scott said.

"No, not much at all."

They headed down the trail and into the silence of the crater. Teri's water bottle, strung to the back of her pack, flapped against her thigh as she walked. *Good. Pound that fat, you little water bottle, you. Break up that cellulite!* She decided she might need to switch sides halfway through so both thighs could come out evenly by the end of the trip.

Once they settled into their individual rhythms of hiking, the group was pretty spread out. She was about four from the back, not too slow and not at all interested in pushing to the lead.

Scott kept pushing forward. He seemed to want her right behind him, but then he would pass someone, which would put a person between them.

Finally, after the third break, she said, "Why don't you go on ahead. I'm doing fine at my own pace."

"But I want you with me," Scott said.

"I'll try to keep up," Teri said with a shrug. "But I can't make any guarantees. This is supposed to be fun, not a race."

That was the wrong thing to say to Scott. Teri realized that, being intensely competitive, he found it hard to make this a leisurely stroll. He was out to conquer the volcano.

"Just go ahead of me," Teri said. "I'll be fine. I'll see you at the cabin or sooner, if we stop for lunch."

"You sure you don't mind?"

"No, have fun. Go knock yourself out. I'm not up for it."

Scott took off without even glancing back. Teri looked at her trail companions: two men younger than she whom she hadn't met until today. "So, are you guys ready to hit the road?"

Her releasing of Scott must have had an effect on the two guys because they began to walk faster. Soon they were a good distance down the trail from Teri, and she realized she was now at the end of the group. This is not what she had wanted. She didn't want to be the weak female who couldn't carry her own weight or keep up with the men. The truth was, they were all in great shape from running around the hotel, hoisting heavy luggage for hours every day. She had been lying around for more than a week with a hurt foot. And it was beginning to feel a little tender now.

Why did I ever come on this trip? I mean, it's beautiful, but I could have seen this from the car and turned around and gone home.

Then slipping into a conversation with God, she prayed, "I certainly hope you have a good reason for bringing me on this journey."

Nineteen

As Teri meandered down the Halemauu Trail, the thought crossed her mind that she had no idea where she was going. She had only half listened when the men mentioned the cabin's name they were planning to stay at tonight.

How hard can this be? I'll stay on the trail until I come to a cabin. They will be there already, kicking back, and they will tease me for being such a slowpoke. I don't care; I plan to enjoy this trip.

She thought of how Gordon had stopped to appreciate the eucalyptus fragrance. That's the way she wanted to experience this adventure, fragrance by fragrance, sight by sight, and sound by sound. The strange thing about the crater was that the deeper in she went, the quieter it became.

How could those guys have gotten ahead of me so fast? I didn't take a wrong turn, did I? I couldn't have. There haven't been any places to turn off. This has to be the right way.

Teri stopped for a drink of water at a curve in the trail. As she stood there, with her foot resting on a pitted volcanic rock, the clouds that had been floating in and out of the center of the crater began to part. The most brilliantly colored rainbow she had ever seen arched before her.

"Oh, Father, it's beautiful!" she whispered. Spontaneously, Teri put down her water bottle and started to applaud while she laughed aloud. Then she watched as the wind drew the cloud curtain over the valley once more, and the rainbow slipped back into the invisible realm. "That was incredible!"

Hitting the dirt road again, Teri whistled to herself her grandmother's favorite hymn, "How Great Thou Art." When she reached the chorus, she sang aloud. Tears formed in her eyes. She couldn't remember the last time she had felt this in love with God. It filled her like nothing else. As the satisfaction seeped into her soul, she wished she had someone to share the moment with.

Then she realized she needed to know that someday Scott could enjoy such a spiritual moment with her. Either Scott had to start showing clear evidence that he was committed to Christ, or she would end their relationship, fireworks or no fireworks.

As the last switchback led to more level, grassy ground, Teri saw a cabin and quickened her step. She could see the guys sitting on the grass, eating and shouting out their "turtle" comments to her as she huffed and puffed their way.

"Tease me all you want," Teri said, unstrapping her pack and lowering it to the ground with a thump, "but I saw a rainbow, and I bet you didn't!"

They all glanced at each other as if to say they had seen so many rainbows in their lifetimes why would one more make a difference?

"This wasn't just any rainbow. It was *the* rainbow of the day, of the week, maybe of the whole year!" She dramatically tossed her hands into the air. "And you speedy burritos missed it."

"Speedy burritos," one of them repeated, and they all laughed.

Teri gave up and sat down next to Scott, who held out to her a stick of beef jerky. "So why aren't we inside the cabin?"

"This isn't the one we're staying at tonight," Dan said.

"Where are we staying, or do I not want to know?" Teri asked.

"Let's just say we're about a third of the way there," Gordon said.

"Which means Teri might make it by sometime around midnight," one of the men teased.

"I can keep up. Don't worry about me."

"Well, time to get going," one of the guys said. "We'll see the rest of you at Kapalaoa Cabin tonight."

Teri took a quick drink of water. "Let's go," she said.

"You need more of a lunch than that," Scott said. "I'll stay with you."

"You don't have to wait. I can eat while I walk."

"You sure?" He reached over and drew a stray curl away from the corner of her mouth.

Teri stood and offered her hand to him as if she had to help him up. He grabbed it, pulled himself up to her, and said, "I can see you hiking the Andes someday. I'd like to go back to Peru. You interested?"

She wondered if anyone else had heard him. All the men were shuffling to put on their packs. "I guess that depends."

"On what?" Scott said, helping her hoist her pack back on. She realized she had felt much more energetic with it off.

"We have a few things we need to talk through," Teri said softly. "I was doing some pretty intense thinking on those switchbacks."

"Oh yeah?" Scott's hair had relaxed from its combed position, and the wayward strands hung over his temples. "That's funny, because I did some intense thinking myself."

The rest of the group tromped on ahead while Scott and Teri hung back to talk.

"I want you in my life, Teri. I've tried to understand what you want. I've tried to take it slow like you asked. I've tried to give you your space. I haven't called every day or hovered over you because I didn't want you to feel smothered."

"I don't feel smothered. I actually feel…well, kind of hurt that you haven't been coming over or calling, especially when I hurt my foot."

Scott shook his head. "Seems we had a misunderstanding, then. I thought you were pushing me away, so I backed off. That's not the way I want things to be. But it's up to you. Are you ready for things to be different?"

Teri hesitated. She thought she was, but being unclear on where Scott stood spiritually was something she wanted to resolve. "May I ask you a few questions?"

"Sure. You mind if we walk as we talk?"

Teri followed him down the trail and said, "Scott, I need to know where you stand with God. I mean, I know you said you became a Christian in high school and that you sort of wandered away in college but now you're ready to get back into church and everything. Well, I guess I want to hear your heart."

"What do you mean?"

"I mean, you know, are you saved? Do you love God? Have you asked Jesus to forgive your sins and come into your heart? Is he the Lord of your life?" Talking to people about spiritual matters had never been Teri's strong point. She suspected her questions were too direct.

Her suspicions were confirmed when Scott started to laugh and said, "Man, what church wouldn't like to make you its Sunday school truant officer!"

"This is important to me, Scott. I want to know how important it is to you."

"Very."

She waited for him to elaborate.

"I believe all the same things you do, babe. Part of the reason I'm so crazy about you is that you're a good influence on me. Are you upset because I haven't gone to church with you yet? You know it's because of my work schedule. As soon as I've been there long enough to ask for a shift change, I'll start going with you. You *are* planning to move here, aren't you?"

"I'm not sure."

"What's to decide? I thought you were going to ask your friend back in Glenbrooke for the tamale business start-up money and get that whole dream in motion. Dan is certainly convinced."

"I do think it's a good idea. It's just that…"

"That you don't know where things stand with me? I think I've made my intentions about as clear as can be. I want you here, babe."

Instead of feeling more secure and stronger about her relationship with Scott, she found herself shrinking back and thinking,

You want me here, but I don't know what I want. It also bothered Teri that he had started to call her "babe." Was that to avoid any more name misunderstandings?

Scott stopped walking and scooped up Teri's hand in his. A sincere expression rested on his handsome face. "Do you remember what I said awhile ago about relaxing and just letting us happen?"

Teri squeezed his hand. "You're right."

He looked into her eyes and in low voice whispered, "Come on, babe. Just let us happen."

Teri let her eyes speak her response. She felt sure Scott would take her in his arms and kiss her. But he didn't. He tightened his grip on her hand and slipped his fingers into her hair. They stood silently in the vastness of the hollow volcano, staring into each other's eyes.

"We better get going," Teri said.

Scott released her hand without a word. She felt a little uncomfortable with the way he mesmerized her, playing her emotions to elicit just the right response. She followed him down the trail and tried to sort out her feelings.

Am I feeling these things naturally, or is Scott somehow manipulating me? Our relationship is so intense. I wish I knew what he was really thinking and feeling. I hear his words, but somehow I don't think I've seen his heart yet.

Teri silently made that her goal. Before this journey was over, she wanted to see Scott's true heart, like Gordon had displayed his when he had said, "Good job, God!" as they were swimming. That's how she wanted to see Scott's.

The trail took a turn at a sign that said Silversword Loop. Gordon stood waiting there for them.

"I'm acting my role as the tour guide," he said. "Have you heard about the silversword yet?"

"I haven't," Teri said.

"Do we have to take this loop?" Scott said. "It looks like the trail goes straight here."

"The loop brings you out on the same trail, but it adds about a quarter mile."

"Let's just keep going," Scott said, forging ahead.

Teri let go of his hand. "I'd like to see this, Scott. I didn't come all this way to miss all the good stuff."

"It's just a bunch of plants. You can see them anywhere."

"Actually," Gordon corrected, "this crater is the only place in the world where the silversword grow. True, they are sprinkled throughout the crater, but this is the most concentrated bunch of them on the planet."

Teri gave Scott an "I told you so" look and turned to join Gordon. "I'm not going to miss this," she said.

Scott reluctantly followed her.

"Right," Gordon said, clearing his throat and beginning his tour-guide speech. "Well, you can see the silverswords at various stages of growth."

"They look like yucca plants," Teri said. She scanned the silver-colored, cactus-like plants scattered around them. Some were tiny sprouts just popping up from the volcanic soil. Others were as tall as she, with a wide variety of sizes between the tiny and the tall.

"Members of the sunflower family, actually."

"Really? They look more like cactus." Teri stopped to look at the silver spikes that stuck out from around the base and curled up. "They look like little porcupines dressed in tutus!" She caught a glimpse of Scott out of the corner of her eye. He looked annoyed.

"These little 'porcupines,'" Gordon continued, apparently unperturbed by her remark, "take anywhere from four years to twenty to grow in that mass of stiletto-shaped leaves. Then, at some mysterious point, they send up a stalk...there, like that one."

"What are all those purple things?"

"The blossoms. They can have more than a hundred blossoms and shoot up to nine feet tall. They bloom only one time. It lasts about a month, and then the plant dies."

"That's amazing," Teri said. "Think of having to wait up to twenty years to bloom and then dying after only a month."

"You make it sound as if you're talking about a person," Scott said, edging on down the trail, trying to lead them onward.

"Oh, that would be tragic," Teri said, automatically falling in line behind Scott. "To wait twenty years to fall in love, only to have it last a month, and then you die."

Scott turned and gave her an "oh, brother" look.

"Come on, Scott!" she teased, swatting at the back of his pack. "Where's your sense of romance?"

"It got tired of waiting around here listening to 'Nature Boy' and ran on ahead of us to the end of the trail." He quickened his pace. "We better try to catch up with it. You wouldn't want me to lose my sense of romance now, would you?"

Teri glanced back at Gordon, who was right behind her. She gave a little shrug and sheepish grin as if to apologize for Scott's comment.

Gordon's intense blue eyes fixed on hers. "I'd wait twenty years," he said just loud enough for her to hear.

Shifting her backpack and focusing on the trail, Teri thought, *Wait twenty years for what? To fall in love? I don't think you have that much time, buddy! Twenty years, and you'll be...*

"Gordon, how old are you?"

"Thirty-four."

Thirty-four sounded old to Teri. She couldn't imagine being thirty-four and not married. Or being thirty-four and saying she would wait twenty more years for the right person. The more she thought about it, the better off she was with Scott.

She allowed herself a leisurely daydream in which she and Scott were married and had two or three kids. They were hiking down this same trail with their little ones. The boys had on hiking boots and were trying hard to keep up with their daddy's long strides. Little Emily, their two-year-old, rode on Scott's shoulders. She had blond hair like her daddy's, and it hung in wild curls like Teri's. In her daydream she was pregnant with their fourth child and healthy and trim as possible for being four months along.

Teri thought about how wonderful it must feel to be pregnant, to carry a tiny life inside that was a part of herself and a little part of...Scott? Scott. Yes, Scott's children would be gorgeous, no doubt.

But could she marry him? Was he really the one? He had certainly made his intentions clear. If only it didn't feel so forced.

Teri watched his hulking frame as he strode down into a valley in the crater that was lined with dark cinders. They crushed shiny black obsidian rocks beneath their feet. He was the essence of strength and confidence. Scott Robinson could have any woman he wanted, and he had chosen Teri.

Come on, Scott, just show me your true heart, and then I'll know for sure.

Twenty

❧

W e were about to send out a search party for you three," Dan said when Teri, Scott, and Gordon finally reached the cabin. It was evening and all the others had obviously been there a long time. Some of the guys were feeding bread to some geese-like birds that had gathered around the front steps of the Kapalaoa Cabin.

"I see the nenes have found you," Gordon said as he pulled off his backpack. "Did you know this is the only place on earth these birds are found?"

Teri heard Scott mutter, "If Nature Boy gives me one more fun fact about this volcano..." Scott's face was red as he clenched his teeth and jerked off his backpack.

For the past several hours Gordon had played his role as tour guide. Scott obviously had become impatient with him. Reaching the cabin had been Scott's goal. Teri, on the other hand, loved hearing all the nature information. But she had stopped asking Gordon questions about an hour ago and, for Scott's benefit, pushed herself to walk faster.

The last hour had seemed longer than the rest of the day put together. While Gordon was talking the time had gone quickly, but Gordon's amiable nature talk was the part that had driven Scott crazy.

"So what's for dinner?" Teri said, hoping to diffuse the tension she felt radiating from Scott.

"We were waiting for you guys," Dan said.

"What? So that I could fix dinner for all of you?" Teri said. "Guess again."

"No, so that we could all eat together," Dan said. "Relax, Teri. I have the spaghetti ready to put in the pot. I didn't want to start it until you arrived."

"Thanks, Dan." She lowered herself to the wooden steps that led to the rustic cabin and released a weary sigh. All the men were looking at her. "What?" she asked, eying them back.

"What took you guys so long?" one of them asked.

"We were enjoying the journey," Teri said. "Did you guys take the Silversword Loop?"

They all looked at each other. "No."

"What is the point of going on a trip like this if you just bull-doze your way to the end of the trail?"

"Beer?" one of them ventured, holding up his half-empty bottle.

"You guys have been holding out on me!" Scott said. "Who was smart enough to pack the Bud?"

Teri watched as Scott opened a bottle of beer and buddied up with the other drinking guys. She didn't think it bothered her that Scott drank. Still, she wasn't sure. Gordon joined them without accepting the beer offered to him. He entered into their conversational circle, and Teri suddenly felt left out. She quietly rose and carried her backpack into the cabin.

It was dark inside. Dan was stirring a pot over a wooden stove at one end of the efficient cabin. A long table filled the center of the room and a bench sat on either side. Along the walls were built-in bunk beds, three levels high. The lower beds already had gear thrown on them.

Teri found an empty bunk on the very top by the door and climbed up to make her bed. She felt a little as if she were at summer camp.

The door opened, and soft evening light poured over Teri's bed. Gordon entered and looked up at her and smiled. "Top perch, aye?"

"I think that's all that's left," she said.

"Could you use a hand, Dan?" Gordon asked.

Teri unfolded her wool blanket and watched the two men trying to wrestle the big pot, which Dan had filled too full of spaghetti noodles. They had to take it outside to pour off the excess water. The minute they exited, the lid on top of the spaghetti sauce began to flutter and then clang. Tomato sauce started to bubble over. Teri scrambled down the side of the bunks and took over in the kitchen, the very thing she had promised herself she wouldn't do.

Dinner turned out fine, with plenty for everyone. She ate quietly, watching the men and the way they interacted with each other. The room was full of individuals. For the most part, they acted as if Teri weren't there, and the topics of discussion were dominated with sports.

Then Dan and Gordon began to talk about being a "one-woman man" with Kai. They talked about being committed for a lifetime to one woman.

Dan, of course, was such a man. Teri wondered about Gordon making such statements, this man with motorcycle scars who opened beer bottles with his teeth. But even more, she wondered about Scott.

Scott must have been thinking of Teri at the same time, because he moved from his spot across the table and came around behind her. In a low, husky voice, he whispered, "Come outside with me."

She felt uncomfortable, making such an obvious exit. As she stood up, Dan turned and gave her a long, hard look. Teri remembered his brotherly advice, and patting him on the shoulder, she said, "Anyone else interested in going for a walk with us?"

No one responded. Teri exited the cabin with Scott, feeling a little less like they were sneaking out.

The minute they closed the door behind them, Scott slid his arm around her waist and said, "Why did you do that?"

"Do what?"

"Invite the rest of them. I asked you to come outside, not them."

"I guess I felt we were being sort of obvious." Scott looked at her, his clear gray eyes waiting for an explanation.

"I just feel funny being the only woman."

"You don't feel uncomfortable being my woman, do you?"

She couldn't answer. Her mind was processing the thought of being the one woman for Scott Robinson.

"Come on," Scott said. "I want to show you something." He led her several hundred yards down the trail to where it was dark and still. Stopping in an open, flat area, Scott took Teri in his arms, pulled her close and began to sway back and forth, humming in her ear.

"What are you doing?" Teri pulled back with a nervous giggle.

"Don't tell me you've never danced under the stars before?"

"I've never danced at all," Teri said.

"Never?"

Teri shook her head.

"You have led a more sheltered life than I realized. Okay. We can deal with this. First, look up."

She did. The black satin sky was alive with twinkling stars. "It's beautiful," she said softly.

"So are you," Scott whispered. "Now put your hand here on my shoulder. That's right. Let me hold your right hand like this. There, now follow my lead." He began to hum and move his feet smoothly back and forth in the sand and gravel beneath them.

Teri tried hard to relax. *This is what you wanted,* she told herself. *Just let us happen. Don't freeze up. He's trying to show you his true heart.*

Scott calmly held her, humming in her ear. Teri felt herself begin to melt. All the rigid rules from her childhood no longer applied. She could dance. Nothing was wrong with dancing. Especially with someone she loved.

I must love him, she told herself. *I wouldn't feel this for him if I didn't love him. This is good. As I loosen up and become a little more like Scott, he'll respond more to me and become a little bit more like me spiritually. That's what Dan was just talking about, blending two lives to make them one.*

"We're really good together," Scott murmured in her ear.

"Don't you think so?"

"Mmm-hmmm," Teri murmured back.

"I don't want to lose you. Tell me that you'll move here so we can start our lives together."

"Okay," Teri said.

Scott stopped dancing and pulled back a few inches to see her face. "Do you really mean it?"

"Yes," she whispered up at him in the shadowy night. "I really mean it." *This is it! The new, improved, no-longer rigid Teri.* "I'm ready to let us happen."

"Good," Scott said, drawing her back to himself, humming again and picking up the dance where he had left off.

Teri could feel her heartbeat echoing off his chest. "You don't mind taking things slowly, do you?" she asked.

"As slow as you want, babe." Scott leisurely took their waltz to an even slower pace. "As slow as you want." Then he bent his head and kissed her on the lips, slowly, gently, and for a long time.

Teri needed no further proof. Scott was the one for her. She was ready to become his woman.

Twenty-One

The sweet dream played itself over and over in Teri's mind the next day as the group hiked down the trail. Dancing with Scott under the stars, deciding to stay on Maui, and being kissed slowly and tenderly were images that waltzed through her mind again and again. No way was she about to analyze the romance out of this.

Scott seemed different from the impatient man of yesterday. Of course, he was in the lead with Teri right behind him, and they weren't stopping at any points of interest to hear "Nature Boy." Instead, Scott and Teri talked freely and with a new openness.

"When we get back," Scott said, "we need to check on a business license for you. But first we need to come up with a name. And open a checking account. Wouldn't hurt to have some business cards made up and some letterhead, too."

"Do you really think this will work?" Teri asked.

"It's worth a try, isn't it? How will you know unless you take the risk?"

Are you talking about the tamale business or our relationship?
Teri realized she wasn't afraid to try either of them, and that felt good.

They hiked only four miles that day. During the last mile or so they tromped on muddy trails through a rain forest in which giant fern jutted from the smooth, black rocks. They were surrounded by towering green foliage, which seemed all the more incredible in contrast to the hot, sandy bleakness of yesterday's trail.

Since the jaunt to the Paliku Cabin was a short one, they arrived in the middle of the day. Rain and water seemed to be everywhere. A card game broke out inside the cabin where they all gathered around the long, wooden table.

Teri lasted for about three hands and then gave up. Cards were another "vice" forbidden in her youth. She was too many years behind the guys to play competitively, so she slung her day pack over her shoulder and ventured outside to explore on her own.

The rain had stopped. The cabin looked dwarfed by the wall of black volcanic rock that had frozen in place on its way from the center of the earth to the ocean. Now the catatonic lava sprouted great, green ferns and wild orchids free for the taking.

With her boots plodding through the mud, Teri walked several yards down the trail. She stopped and looked up. Two perfect rainbows arched over her in the clearing sky of the late afternoon.

The sight made Teri catch her breath. Yet no one was around to share this glorious moment. She wished Scott were there, standing with her. At a moment like this she would hear his true heart. He would wrap his arms around her, and she would feel warm and secure.

As it was, she felt lonely. Not at all like she had felt when she had applauded and sang aloud to God yesterday on discovering the rainbow.

What's changed in me? I don't even feel as if I'm the same person I was yesterday.

Softly, she began to hum the song that had helped to express her jubilation yesterday. She forced the words to her lips. Finally the song tumbled out reluctantly and plunged to the ground. "How great Thou art…"

A rich baritone from somewhere above her added, "then sings my soul…"

Teri spun around and spotted Gordon crouched on the hillside among the ferns and orchids. "I remember hearing my grandmother sing that one," he called down to her.

Teri smiled. The song must have been the favorite of grannies around the world. "Mine, too," she called back.

Gordon plucked a flower and galloped down the steep hill. Teri winced as she watched, certain he would fall. Miracle of miracles, Gordon made it down in one piece, and with such a light step that he left little evidence of having been on the hillside.

He strode toward Teri. She stood still, watching the way he confidently approached. He had attacked the waves that day on the beach with the same exuberance.

Stepping close to Teri, he held out the flower. That crazy, laughing look was on his face. "Some take only a few days to bloom."

"Not like the silversword," Teri said, remembering the botany lesson from the day before.

"Strange, isn't it? The flowers don't resist blooming at their appointed time. Why do we?"

Teri accepted the flower from him and traced her finger across the delicate petals. She wasn't sure she understood what he meant. "Is this what you call the 'unforced rhythm of grace'?"

Gordon looked surprised at her words. "Right! Where did you hear that?"

"Annie. She told me about your creative communion service."

He broke into a cascade of laughter. "Frail humans we are, fumbling with the eternal. I can't wait until the day when we meet at his table, that great marriage feast of the Lamb."

"Gordon…" He was still standing rather close, and she hesitated to look up at him.

"I shall run into his open arms," Gordon said, absorbed in his thoughts of heaven.

"Gordon?" she said again, looking at him and waiting until he looked back at her. "May I ask you something?"

"Of course. Anything."

"Do you think I should marry Scott?"

Gordon moved back nearly a foot. He didn't answer right away. Then, clearing his throat, he said, "I'm afraid my opinion is rather biased."

"So? Tell me." His "baptismal" skills as a pastor were a little rough, but Teri thought he seemed like a tender, honest counselor. She wanted to hear his opinion.

Stretching out one arm, Gordon wrapped it around Teri's shoulder and gave her a friendly squeeze. "This is with one arm," he said. Then he encircled her with both his arms, drawing her close in an embrace so tight and so strong that it took her breath away. "This," he murmured in her ear, "is with two arms." Then, as instantly as he had hugged her, he let go and stepped back.

Teri caught her breath.

"The real question, Teri, is this: Does Scott embrace your heart with one arm or two? Answer that, and you'll know."

She felt her cheeks flush and didn't look at Gordon. Instead of giving her helpful counsel, he had confused her.

"Thanks," she mumbled. "I'll give it some thought."

A smile crept up Gordon's face. "He's the wild one, you know."

"You mean Scott?"

"No." Gordon laughed. "God. His ways aren't our ways. His thoughts aren't our thoughts. He just might surprise you, surprise both of us."

Teri certainly agreed. She confessed to Gordon that not many events in her life had gone the way she had thought they would. But she had seen God's presence in each situation, if not during the decision-making process, then certainly afterwards. She could look back and find his fingerprints all over the circumstances.

Gordon smiled and said, "That's the way then, isn't it, Teri? To look for God's fingerprints. I like that. We must do that. Watch for his fingerprints."

"I suppose you're right," Teri said, turning an opened palm to the sky as she realized it was starting to rain again. "We should probably get back."

They sloshed together though the mud to the cabin and found the card game still going. No one seemed to have noticed that they came in together.

No one, not even Scott, saw her place the orchid between

several facial tissues and gently step on it with her heavy boot. She slipped the flattened, tissue-wrapped flower into the only safe travel place she could think of, the bottom of the small pack of Kleenex, against the thin piece of cardboard.

Teri thought about Gordon's strange word picture and wondered if she had offered Scott a two-armed embrace. She was always holding back. She called it being careful, Scott called it rigid. Teri determined to extend to Scott a two-armed approach.

That evening, after dinner, they all sat around the table talking. She leaned against Scott and lifted his arm so that it encircled her. Scott willingly drew her close and, in front of the others, whispered into her hair. The attention was exhilarating.

The rest of the group treated them differently on the third day as they set out on their long hike back. Everyone assumed the two of them wanted to be alone, since they were making it clear they were a couple. The men were ready early that morning, before Teri had finished loading her pack, and so the others took off. Scott was ready, too. But he stayed behind, waiting for Teri. She quickly twisted a bandanna and turned it into a headband to hold back her wild and now dirty hair.

"Aren't you about ready?" Scott asked as she tied the laces on her boots. "Come on."

"I'm ready, I'm ready," Teri said cheerfully, strapping on her pack.

"It's a killer hike today, babe. Come on. They're not going to want to wait around for us at the cars."

"Let's go," Teri said, briskly sliding past him and opening the cabin door. It was raining again. According to Gordon's information, the average rainfall at this cabin was 250 inches or more a year. "Wait! I forgot to put on my rain poncho."

Now Scott was looking impatient. He kept that expression for the next three, long, soggy hours. By the time they were back into the sun-baked bowl of the crater, neither of them was in a good mood.

Scott looked as if he were even more perturbed when they spotted Gordon standing at one of the "points of interest."

"Oh, great," Scott sputtered. "Nature Boy is waiting."

"Scott," Teri said quietly, "he's only trying to be helpful."

"He bugs me. The guy doesn't know when to let up! Did you hear him singing this morning?"

Teri had thought waking up to Gordon's singing as he had made breakfast for everyone was nice. He wasn't singing loud. It was sort of like his laughter; the music tumbled out of him. She had heard him humming and whistling several times on the trip. "Be nice, okay, Scott?"

"And what do we have here, oh great Kahuna of the Crater?" Scott called out to Gordon. Teri could tell the teasing was not good-natured.

"The bottomless pit," Gordon said. He was standing beside a railing that circled a hole about ten feet wide on the black volcano floor. "Sixty-five feet to the bottom."

"Are you sure?" Scott said. "Can't we try throwing something in to test it?"

Teri was afraid that Scott's idea of "something" was Gordon himself. Scott kept walking past the scenic spot as if he had no intention of slowing down.

"Traditionally, it's dried umbilical cords that go in."

"Wait a second," Teri said. "I have to hear this one."

"Go ahead," Scott said. "I have to keep going. If I break my stride now, I know I'll cramp up. I'm sure you two can catch up with me in a few minutes."

Teri watched him go and then turned her surprised face back to Gordon. She had forgotten what Gordon had said and why she had stopped. It was one thing for Scott not to hike with her on the first day of their trip. But now they were together. They were a couple. How could he leave her like this?

Gordon met Teri's gaze, his steel blue eyes didn't move from hers. Somehow she felt calmed.

"I'm sorry, Gordon. What were you saying?"

Instead of continuing his tour guide speech, he gave Teri a sympathetic look. "You all right?" he asked.

"Me? Sure. Yeah. I'm fine." She pushed a smile onto her lips. "What was it you said about this hole? Sixty-five feet or something?"

"Right. In ancient times, the Hawaiian men would come all this way to toss in the umbilical cords of their newborns. Only their sons, I think. How many children do you want?"

"Children? How many do I want?"

"How many children do you want?" Gordon repeated.

Teri shook herself from her dazed state and answered, "Four. Maybe five."

Gordon smiled and turned to head back up the main trail. He lost his balance for a second, and Teri lurched forward to grab his arm. They both steadied the other, only a foot away from the bottomless pit.

"That wasn't funny," Teri snapped. "We could have landed on a pile of petrified umbilical cords."

Gordon broke into laughter.

"Come on," Teri said. "Let's catch up with the others."

They marched up the trail silently for quite some time, breathing hard from the ascent. Suddenly Gordon said, "I think four is good. I'd like even numbers. Six would be better than five."

Teri had no idea what he was talking about and was too winded to ask.

CHAPTER

Twenty-Two

❧

Teri sat alone in the sand and watched the early morning waves rush toward the shore. The beach was deserted except for a few early-rising beachcombers. Three days had passed since she had returned from the hike through the crater, and she was still sore. Everywhere.

This morning she had borrowed the car, promising to be back by 8:30. She needed to get out of the house and away from everything and everyone to try to think things through.

Tracing her finger in the cool sand, Teri mentally listed her issues as if she were listing Spanish verbs on the board for her class to conjugate. Because most verbs were easy since they followed the rules, her students viewed the exercise as boring. That is, until she sprinkled in the irregular verbs, the ones that didn't follow any rules or fit any logical patterns. The correct answer for those verbs could only be learned by memorization.

This morning Teri would give anything to know the correct answers to the "irregular verbs" in her life. She didn't know the right responses. She had no experience that would enable her to memorize them. And her most pressing questions didn't seem to follow any pattern.

First irregular question: Was she doing the right thing by moving to Maui? Last night, with Dan's help, Scott had formulated a plan for Teri. She would fly back to Oregon on her scheduled flight Thursday. In the next ten days she would cancel her teaching contract for the fall, give notice to her landlord, sort through all her belongings, pack only what she absolutely needed, and return to Maui. They were still working through the details of the business license. Oh, and she would secure the needed start-up money as a loan from her wealthy friend, Jessica.

"Is that what you want me to do, God?"

She waited for a thunderous clap of lightening to affirm her decision. All she heard were the steady waves. They ran to her, unrolling their foaming scrolls at her feet. But no words were written on the waters that could answer her question. Or at least none that she could read.

Teri ventured to ask the next question. "Father, do you want me to make this commitment to Scott?" She listened carefully to the morning winds, gusting their way to the farthest oceans. But to their powerful language, she was a foreigner.

With a sigh of exhaustion, Teri flung one final petition into the morning air. "Lord, what do you want me to do?"

Nothing. No answer. No sign.

All she could think of was Gordon. She smiled, remembering when Gordon had said, "He's the wild one, you know."

"The wild one," she whispered back to the wind and waves. "But then, you knew that, didn't you?" She was thinking of the familiar account of when Jesus commanded the waves and the wind to be still. Only the one who was wilder than the wind and the waves could do that.

Teri stood and dusted off the seat of her jeans. She stretched her stiff legs and headed back to the car. *What a wonderful, spiritual morning, she thought.*

She felt spiritually exhilarated ever since the strenuous hike out of the crater. Scott had kept pace with the other guys at the lead, and Gordon had stayed behind with Teri. She had a hard time admitting to herself, let alone anyone else, that Gordon's company had been the highlight of the trip. He had given her a lot to think about.

She also had thought about Dan's comment that she and Annie had grown up in the fish bowl of ministry life and had become conditioned to live in a way acceptable to the people who were always watching them. It fit with the way Scott told her to stop apologizing and saying she was sorry all the time.

She found all this a lot to digest in a few days, especially on top of the pressing questions about her future. She had hoped to process some of her thoughts this morning, but now, here she was, leaving the beach with more questions rather than less. All she could think of was how much she wanted to talk to Gordon, to hear his pastoral counsel even if it did come across in crazy riddles. At least he helped her to think.

Back at the house, Teri scanned the church phone directory on the counter until she found Gordon's number. She dialed it, not exactly sure what she was going to say. After eleven rings, she gave up.

Now Teri didn't know what to do. Maybe she could talk things through with Scott. She tried his number, but his answering machine responded to her call.

"Scott, it's me. Call me as soon as you can. I really need to talk. I know you said last night that you would be over this evening around five, but if we could get together before then, it would be great. Bye."

All she could do was wait. The day inched along at a snail's pace. Close to five Scott called to say he was hung up and wouldn't be able to come by. He didn't give a clear reason.

"Did you get tomorrow morning off work so you can go to church with me?" Teri asked. She hated the twinge of a whine she heard in her voice.

"Ah, yes and no. I got off work, but I agreed to take some people sailing. It's the only time they can go. I knew you would understand."

Teri did understand. Perhaps she was too understanding. She also understood when Scott called Sunday afternoon to say he was too tired to come over and promised to see her Monday evening. She said she understood when he showed up late Monday, and she, Dan, and Annie were almost finished eating. Scott acted as if everything were just fine as he ate his warmed up dinner and talked over business finances with Dan.

When Teri finally had a moment alone with Scott, she was steamed.

"You realize, don't you, that I'm leaving in three days."

"Only for a week and a half. Then you'll be back for good."

"Maybe," Teri said.

"What do you mean 'maybe'? That's what you promised me. You agreed to move here, remember?"

"It's a huge decision, Scott. The last few days I've been really struggling with it, and I haven't seen you or been able to talk with you. To be honest, I'm not convinced it's the right decision for me."

Scott tilted his head and fixed his gray eyes on her. Storm clouds seemed to appear in them. "What are you saying, Teri?"

"I don't know."

"Can I make it any more clear to you? I want you here. With me."

His words echoed in her fitful sleep that night and the next morning while she and Annie shopped in Lahaina. Teri wanted to take home a few souvenirs and had convinced Annie to walk down Front Street with her to poke around all the little tourist shops.

It turned out to be a good activity for the two sisters. They took their time and even lingered over a light lunch at one of the cafés. The conversation mostly centered around the baby and the tamale business.

"I'm glad you're coming back to stay," Anita said as they drove back home. "It'll be good to have you here."

Teri wasn't sure if Anita's comments were sincere or if perhaps she had picked up on Teri's lack of confidence and was doing a little fishing. Teri had almost opened up to Gordon at church Sunday. She had spoken to him briefly and had wanted to ask his advice on the big decisions in her life, but Anita was standing there with them so Teri had said nothing.

Staring out the car's window at the lush, west Maui mountains, Teri thought she was being paranoid again. Annie wanted her here. Scott wanted her here. Gordon had even said something about looking forward to her being here when he returned from seminary at Christmas time. Dan couldn't wait to start the tamale business. She was the only one who had cold feet. *Here I go again, analyzing all the adventure out of my life.*

They drove down Scott's street on the way home, and Teri

noticed his car out front. "Stop here, Annie. Scott's home. I want to surprise him. I'll have him bring me home later."

Anita slowly pulled over to the side of the road. "Teri, I've been wanting to tell you something."

Teri's hand was on the door handle, about to open it and hop out. She looked at her sister impatiently, prepared to defend herself or defend Scott, as she usually did. "What?"

"Dan said that on the backpack trip he and some guys were talking about the baby and everything. One of the guys was Scott." Anita paused.

"So?" Teri could feel her temper flaring. How dare Anita try to toss in some poisoned seeds about Scott just before Teri saw him? Why didn't Anita bring any of this up over lunch? "What's your point?"

"Dan said that Scott made it clear he didn't want to have any children. Ever."

"What does that have to do with anything?"

"I thought you should know," Anita snapped.

"Okay, now I know." Teri got out and stomped up to the front door. *Why does she do that to me? Just because she knows I want to have a bunch of kids someday, she has to needle me about some stupid thing Scott supposedly said. I was there, and I didn't hear him say anything like that.*

Teri knocked briskly on the door frame as she tried to see through the mesh on the screen door. "Scott?" she called out.

A young, slender blond wearing a backless sundress stepped out of the kitchen and came to the door. "Hi," she said.

Teri stared at her. "Is Scott here? I saw his car and I…"

"No, he's at work. We traded cars today. Do you want to

leave a message for him or anything?"

"No," Teri said, backing up. "That's okay. Thanks."

She turned to go, but her shock and curiosity wouldn't let her walk away. She looked back at the gorgeous woman who was still standing behind the screen door. Allowing her grit to kick in, Teri asked, "By the way, what's your name?"

"Julie. Do you want me to tell Scott you stopped by?"

"No," Teri muttered under her breath as she turned to go. "Don't bother."

Twenty-Three

❧

Y ou win!" Teri shouted, storming into the house and slamming the screen door behind her. "You were right all along, Annie. Go ahead and gloat."

Anita was on the phone in the kitchen. She tucked her head and covered her free ear with her hand. "Yes, she's right here," Anita said and held out the phone to Teri. "It's Scott."

"I don't want to talk to him!" Teri said.

"He says it's important." Anita held out the phone.

"Oh, I bet it is."

"What am I doing?" Anita said into the air. "I'm not getting in the middle of this!" She plopped the receiver onto the counter and walked away with her hands up in surrender. "I just live here," she sputtered. "I don't know what's going on, and I don't want to know!" She slipped into her bedroom and closed the door hard.

Teri stared at the receiver, which was rocking on the kitchen counter. She could hear Scott's muffled voice.

Feeling like a volcano was about to erupt inside her, Teri

grabbed the phone and shouted, "I don't think you have any-thing to say to me, Scott Robinson, that could ever change my opinion of you!"

"What is your problem?" he shouted back.

"*My* problem? You're the one with the problem!"

"What are you raving about?"

"I'll tell you what I'm raving about." She tried to lower her voice and gain some kind of emotional control. "I stopped by your house because I saw you car and guess who answered the door?"

Scott didn't respond.

"*Julie* answered the door."

"So?"

"So, she acted like she lived there!"

"She does," Scott said.

Teri dropped into the nearest chair. Her mind was boggled.

"Julie is Bob's girlfriend. She moved in a couple of weeks ago. Didn't I tell you?"

"Bob's girlfriend?" Teri felt as if someone had punched her in the stomach.

"Yeah, Bob's girlfriend. Are you having a bad hormone day or something?"

Teri didn't answer.

"Are you still there?"

"Yes," Teri said in a small voice.

"I was calling to tell you that our dinner reservations are at seven."

"Seven," Teri repeated, her voice still as small as a mouse's.

"Okay," Scott said in an even voice, regaining control. "Seven. I'll pick you up around 6:30. It's a nice place so you might want to dress up a little."

"Okay," Teri said. "Scott, I…" She was about to say she was sorry but then remembered how much that irritated him.

"I'm looking forward to seeing you."

"I'm looking forward to seeing you too," he said and hung up.

Teri sat still for a long time. Her brain had turned to mush, and her emotions were skittering on the edge of a deep precipice. Anita inched her way out of her room and pulled up a chair next to Teri's. She sat there, waiting for Teri to speak.

"Is this what love does? Makes you crazy?" Teri finally said in a monotone voice.

"It's supposed to heal you," Anita said softly.

"It's me," Teri said, the tears finally forming in her glazed eyes. "I'm no good at relationships. You said it yourself. I analyze all the romance out. Scott says I'm rigid and paranoid. He's right."

"It's not you, Teri," Anita said in a firm yet gentle voice. "When the right man enters your life, you'll know. It won't be like this."

"The right man? Scott is the right man for me. There will never be anyone more perfect than Scott. He's any woman's dream come true."

"Then let any woman have him," Anita said, picking up steam. "He's not the right man for you. Think about it, Teri! Open your eyes for one minute and look at what this relationship with Scott has done to you. You're not being yourself. You're performing for this man, trying to be what he expects you to be. That's not love. It's a bunch of games. Why are you afraid of letting go of this relationship? It's not healthy."

Teri was too exhausted to argue. "Just leave me alone."

Anita stood up but didn't leave. She seemed to be ready to say something and then changed her mind and walked off.

Teri forced herself up and went into the bathroom where she stood a long time in the steaming, hot shower. *I'll just play it out. That's all I can do. I'll go to dinner and see what happens. I can't listen to Annie or anyone else. I have to call this one. I'll be able to tell after tonight.*

Scott arrived on time, looking the best Teri had ever seen him. His clothes were casual island-wear, but nothing was casual about the way he looked her over. She wore a sundress that scooped in the front and showed off her bronzed summer skin. When she had put it on, Teri had scrutinized her reflection in the mirror, criticizing herself for not looking as sleek and youthful as Julie had in her backless sundress. But for Teri, this was about as daring as she got. Apparently Scott liked it.

"Hey, beautiful," he said, reaching for her elbow and drawing her close. "Are you ready to go?"

Teri looked up at him and smiled. He smelled clean, like the wind off the ocean. He had to be the most handsome man she had ever seen. And he was with her, holding her, whispering to her, taking her out to dinner. All of her tangled emotions began to smooth out, and the fantasy came back into view.

He drove into Lahaina with his arm across the back of the seat, his fingers woven into her cascading curls. Mellow jazz floated from his car stereo, and neither of them spoke. Teri surmised that this is how things would be once they were married.

Their conflicts were all based in a lack of communication and the confusion she felt when they were apart. As long as they were together, like this, nothing could divide them. Teri decided that the sooner they were married, the better. That would silence their critics. As a matter of fact, if she could marry him right this instant, she would.

"I thought about you all day." Scott's voice was a low rumble, blending with the music. "This is going to be a perfect evening for us." His hand broke through her thick mane, and his strong fingers massaged her neck.

"That feels good," Teri said, her voice barely above a purr.

"I take it you're feeling a little better than you did when I called this afternoon?"

Her eyes met his as he quickly glanced over. "I owe you an apology, Scott. I was out of line. Thanks for being so under-standing."

She could see his lips curl into a smile. "No problem," he said. Then drawing back his arm, he used both hands to turn the wheel into a tight parking spot on Front Street. "You ever been to Kimos?"

"Last summer. Did you know that Dan works here on Friday nights?"

Scott opened her door and offered his hand to help her out. "I might be working here on Friday nights," he said. "They cut back my hours at Halekuali'i. Can you believe it? Sixteen hours a week doing valet parking and twenty-four running room service. Not exactly enough to pay the bills. The sooner we get the tamales going, the better."

The block of sidewalk between the car and the restaurant was thick with tourists. Yet, in the sea of all those people, the first face

Teri saw was Mark Hunter's. He was walking toward them with his arm around a petite, dark-haired woman, and he noticed Teri too.

"Hi." Teri spoke first, stopping in the middle of the sidewalk and smiling at Mark. "Scott, you remember Mark, don't you? Mark Hunter, Scott Robinson."

The two men amiably exchanged greetings.

"This is Claire," Mark said. "Claire, this is Teri and Scott."

The two women greeted one another.

After that no one seemed to know what to say. Dozens of pedestrians walked around them.

"We were just headed for Kimos," Scott said, tugging on Teri's hand as a hint that he wanted to get going.

"Dan told me you're leaving this week," Mark said quickly. He was looking at Teri as if no one else were around.

"In two days," Teri said, her gaze fixed on Mark. She hated this clenched up feeling in her stomach, the feeling that things were still unresolved between them.

"Excuse me," Mark said, removing his arm from around Claire's shoulders. "Scott, Claire, would you mind if I spoke privately with Teri for just a moment?"

Scott didn't let go of Teri's hand at the same time that she let go of his. She glanced over at Scott, and he released his grip, saying, "I'll go on to the restaurant and see if our table is ready."

"I'll be inside this shop, Mark," Claire said. She smiled at Teri. "I'm glad to meet you, Teri. Mark has spoken highly of you." She slipped into the shop filled with T-shirts and beach towels.

Teri felt herself begin to blush as she looked up.

Mark moved to the side of the building, to allow pedestrians to walk unblocked on the sidewalk. "Teri, I wanted to call you. I was going to. Actually, I was going to stop by and see you. But this is better. I've been wanting to tell you thanks for, well...I guess for being so direct that morning at breakfast."

Teri could tell Mark was struggling to form so many words so quickly and be so open. She guessed he had practiced these sentences more than once.

"I want you to know that last summer was really special for me," he continued. "I enjoyed being with you, and I'll always have great memories of our time together. And I meant every word I said in my letters and phone calls during this past year. I was eager to see you this summer. And then you got here and..."

"I know," Teri said. "It just wasn't the same. That's nobody's fault. Relationships change. Claire seems like a wonderful woman for you."

"But that's what I wanted to tell you," Mark said. "I couldn't see that. For months she and I worked together, and I never thought of her as anything more than a research partner because I was waiting for you. She knew that. Then when things didn't fall back into place with you and me, I felt bad. After you released me that morning, I finally saw that I'd been holding on to a sort of illusion about us. Do you know what I mean?"

Teri nodded.

"Then it's like I saw Claire for the first time. I wanted you to know that I wasn't going out behind your back or anything. I know we didn't have any kind of commitment to each other, but I think we both wanted to wait and see what would happen."

"You're right," Teri said. "I don't know why some relationships only last for a season."

"That doesn't make them any less real or any less important. You taught me to lighten up, Teri. You saw the joy in every situation, and I'm the better for having cared about you."

"You'll always hold a little corner of my heart too, Mark. Thanks for telling me all this."

Mark reached for her hand and gave it a squeeze. She squeezed his back, and the two friends exchanged smiles.

"Teri," Scott called from down the street. He put his two fingers between his teeth and gave a shrill whistle.

"I guess our table is ready," Teri said. "God bless you, Mark."

"He has," Mark said, giving her a quick hug. "And God bless you, Teri."

She turned and gave a friendly wave to Claire, who was nonchalantly watching from inside the store. Claire blushed at being caught and returned the wave.

Edging her way through the crowds, Teri hurried to the restaurant. Inside she glowed. *What a man of integrity. How funny that he said I taught him to lighten up. I must have changed. Now I'm the one who's always uptight. Is it me? Or is it the way I act around Scott, like Annie says? I'd say it's time I started to find the joy in every situation again.*

"Come on," Scott grasped her by the elbow. "Our table is ready."

"That was the best five minutes I could ever have spent, Scott," Teri said, trying to convey her joy as the hostess led them to their window table. "I feel so good about everything now."

Scott pulled out her chair, and the hostess handed her a menu. "Thank you," Teri said. "I was really unsettled about how everything sort of ended up with Mark, and now it's clear and open. I'm so happy!"

Scott reached over and tipped down the top of her menu. "What are you telling me? Did you date that guy?"

"Last summer. Didn't I tell you?"

Scott did not look pleased. "You're saying you and that guy had something going last summer?"

"Something going?" Teri repeated with a laugh. "I guess, if that's what you want to call it. We spent some time together. Exchanged a few letters over the year. A few phone calls."

"And have you been seeing him this summer? Going out with him the same time you've been going out with me?"

"No, of course not. Well," Teri quickly caught herself, "we did meet for breakfast one morning, but that was just to talk and figure out where our relationship was going."

Scott raised his eyebrows with a critical glare, indicating for her to continue. "It's going nowhere, Scott. That's what I'm trying to tell you. You're acting like I've been two-timing you or something!" Now Teri was frustrated. "I should never have said anything. The whole point was that when we met for breakfast I did all the talking. I said I didn't want to pursue the relationship. He didn't say anything then, but he told me tonight that he agreed. He's with Claire. Didn't you see how happy they looked together? You're not getting this, are you?"

Scott lifted his menu and didn't say anything. Teri tried not to let the joy she had felt slip away. Maybe Scott was jealous, the way she had felt jealous of Julie. But there was nothing for him to be jealous of, just as there had been nothing for her to be jealous of with Julie. She tried to tell him.

He lowered his menu and said, "Let's forget the whole thing and start over." He smiled, and she felt a little better.

"The fish sounds good," Scott said, scanning the menu. "Do you know what you'd like?"

They both were barricaded behind their menus when the waiter arrived at the table. A voice with a definite Australian accent said "Good evening. Would you like to hear about our specials?"

Twenty-Four

Gordon? When did you start working here?" Teri asked, laying down her menu and smiling at their waiter.

"Well, Teri and Scott," he said. "This is great! My first night on the job, and I get to practice on friends. Let's see now," Gordon began to read the specials off the pad in his hand. "We have fresh ahi grilled with a lemon butter sauce…"

Teri glanced at Scott. He didn't look too thrilled. *What makes Scott feel such animosity toward Gordon?*

Gordon finished his list and looked to Teri for a response. "I'll have the mahimahi," she said. "It's my favorite."

"Mine too," Gordon replied, writing down the order. "And for you, Scott?"

"Prime rib. End cut. Butter and sour cream on the potato."

"Great! I'll be back in a bit with your salads." Gordon took their menus, and looking at Teri, he said, "You look gorgeous tonight."

She smiled her thanks, watching him until he was gone, and then turned her attention to Scott. He had that jealous frown on his face again.

A woman in a tight wraparound dress sauntered past their table with a basket of corsages and leis. "Flowers?" she asked softly.

Teri could smell the heady, sweet fragrance and looked over the assortment. "They're beautiful," she said, anticipating that Scott would take the hint. "What are those little white ones?" She pointed to a lei strung with slender, white buds.

"Tuberose," she answered.

Teri waited for Scott to respond and buy the lei for her. He didn't. His dark mood seemed to engulf him. Without acknowledging the saleswoman, he said to Teri, "What are you tonight? A man-magnet?"

"What are you talking about?"

The flower girl discretely slipped away.

"First Mark out on the street and now Gordon looking at you as if you're the only woman in the place."

"What is with this jealousy thing with you, Scott? You didn't mind my being around Gordon in the crater. In fact, you left me with him for hours."

"Only because you wanted to lag behind and hear all his stupid stories."

"His stories are not stupid. Gordon knows a lot about the environment. I was trying to learn something." Teri felt her temper flare and didn't notice the flower vendor returning to their table.

"Excuse me," she said. "This is for you." She placed the tuberose lei over Teri's head. "Compliments of your waiter."

Scott immediately reached for his wallet. "How much is it? I'll pay for it," he said.

"It's already paid for," she said and strolled over to the next table, tilting her basket in their direction.

Teri drew in the intense, sweet fragrance.

Scott looked as if he were about to say something when Gordon stepped up to the table and set their salads before them. "Ground pepper?" he asked, holding the mill above Teri's plate.

"Just a little. Thanks for the flowers. They're beautiful. And so fragrant!"

"Glad you like them," Gordon said, giving the pepper mill a twist. "Pepper for you, Scott?"

He still looked mad. "Sure," he mumbled, without looking at Gordon.

Gordon lifted the pepper mill over Scott's salad. Before he could give it a twist, the metal plate on the bottom fell off, landing in Scott's salad along with a mound of black pepper.

"Whoa!" Gordon quickly tilted the mill, sprinkling pepper in Scott's face as Gordon tried to stop the flow. "So sorry, there. My mistake." He scooped up the plate and said, "I'll be right back with another salad for you."

Scott swatted at his lap and the table with his cloth napkin. "Jerk," he muttered.

"It was an accident," Teri said softly. "It wasn't his fault."

"Yeah, well he tends to attract accidents, in case you haven't noticed."

"I know," Teri said, suppressing a giggle. "He took me with him into the ocean a couple of weeks ago when he tripped off the rocks."

"When was this? You never told me."

Teri relayed the incident, explaining that she had gone to the beach to think and had run into Gordon. "He called it a divine appointment," she said with a laugh.

"You sure you two didn't plan to meet there? You weren't arranging a talk with him like your breakfast with that other guy?"

"Of course not!"

"It sounds to me like you were pretty busy meeting other men these past few weeks. Here I thought I was giving you your space, time to think through our relationship."

"I can't believe you're saying these things, Scott!"

Gordon stepped up with a fresh salad.

"No pepper this time," Scott said curtly.

Gordon, appearing undaunted, nodded his head and went on to the next table.

"You didn't have to be so rude," Teri said.

"I wasn't rude." Scott jabbed his fork into his salad and took a bite. "I don't know why you're so determined to start a fight tonight."

"Me? I'm not trying to start a fight!"

Scott took another bite of salad and said, "Why aren't you eating?"

"I usually pray before I eat." Then softening her tone, she said, "Scott, could you pray for us? I think we could use it right now."

Scott lowered his fork and swallowed. "You go ahead," he said, respectfully waiting for her to pray.

"I'd like it if you would," she said. "I feel a man should take the lead, especially in spiritual matters."

"You're stuck in your childhood again," Scott said. "Men and women are equal. They should approach a relationship, spiritually and otherwise, on an equal level."

"Never mind," Teri said. "We don't have to pray."

"No, you go ahead," Scott said. "It doesn't bother me."

"That's the problem, Scott. It doesn't bother you a bit."

"What's that supposed to mean?"

"Nothing. Never mind. Let's eat in peace, okay?"

Scott picked up his fork and went at his salad with gusto, not saying a word. Teri squeezed her eyes shut and silently prayed. *Oh, Father, what am I doing? Scott is not the right man for me. How did I ever talk myself into this? Show me what you want for me. Set things straight.*

She opened her eyes and the first thing she saw was Gordon's hand delivering a basket of fresh rolls. "How are your salads?" he asked.

"Fine," Teri said, trying to act as if nothing were wrong.

"Great. I'll go check on your dinners."

"Scott," Teri began a few moments later, "I'm not sure things are working out for us."

"Come on, babe," he said, his smooth, confident tone returning. "All couples have their disagreements. Just let it go, all right?"

Teri shook her head. "Scott, we're too different."

"Are you getting hung up about the racial thing again?"

"No, I mean different in here," she tapped her heart. "I think we should be equal, like you said. I guess I just realized we don't have an equal embrace between our hearts. I mean, we've both tried. I know you have, and I know I have. It's just that it seems

188

so forced. If we're seriously planning on getting married—"

"Getting married?" Scott said and started to laugh.

Gordon was suddenly standing beside the table, holding their dinners.

"Where did you get the idea I was thinking of us getting married?"

Teri felt embarrassed that Gordon was hearing this. She scooted her salad plate to the side and made room for the steaming mahimahi Gordon placed before her.

"And prime rib, end cut," he said, delivering the platter to Scott.

"I need some horseradish," Scott said, without acknowledging Gordon's presence. "And some more sour cream."

"Right," Gordon said. "Anything else for you, Teri?"

She didn't look up but said, "Could you please bring me a glass of iced tea?"

He vanished, and Scott reached across the table and grasped Teri's hand. "Hey, I don't know what's been going on in that head of yours, but these past few weeks, I've been talking about us getting together. You know, taking it step by step. I didn't plan for you to move here so we could get married. Decisions like that take a lot of time. It's a huge commitment. We're not there yet."

Teri started to feel the fog of confusion float in and cloud her reasoning as it had many times during the past few weeks. Scott was right. They needed to take things slowly. Isn't that what she had said from the beginning? Why did she ever think he wanted to marry her?

Scott let go of her hand and a bit of his magic dust left her. "While you're packing up your things next week I'll be looking for a place for us. It'll be different once you're back here for good and we're together all the time."

"A place for us?" Teri said. "You mean, like move in together?"

"Of course. You can't make the tamales in your sister's house. She said she couldn't stand the smell."

Out of the corner of her eye, Teri saw Gordon carrying a tray toward them. In a low voice she said, "Scott, I can't move in with you."

"Why not?"

"Because I...I..."

"If we're going to give our relationship a fair try," Scott said, "we have to go all the way."

His choice of words caused Teri to feel panic rise up inside.

"The only way we'll know if it's going to work is if we move in together."

Gordon heard that. She knew he did. Teri didn't want to look at him. He placed the ramekin of horseradish on the table. She shyly peeked up as he removed the ramekin of sour cream from the tray in his hand. Teri noticed her glass of iced tea begin to slide off the tray, but before she could say anything, the iced tea hit the edge of the tray, tipped and poured its icy waterfall into Scott's lap.

"You jerk!" Scott shouted, jumping up and looking as if he were about to slug Gordon. "That does it! Tell your manager I want to talk to him. No, wait. Better yet, I'll go talk to him." Scott pushed Gordon away with one arm and, with a restaurant full of spectators, marched in his wet pants to the front desk.

Teri buried her face in her hands. She couldn't believe what a disaster this night had turned into.

"Teri," Gordon's voice sounded soothing. She peeked between her fingers and didn't see him.

"Teresa," he repeated.

She removed her hands, and there was Gordon, down on one knee by her chair. His face looked sincere, his demeanor undaunted by either the spill or the fear of what would come next for him when Scott finished with the manager.

"My timing may not be the best, but Teri I have to tell you I'm in love with you. I don't know how to say this any other way. Teresa, will you marry me?"

She stared at him along with two dozen other people seated around them. "Gordon," she said with a nervous laugh. "People are watching."

"So are the angels," he said, unmoved.

Teri laughed her nervous laugh again. She shot apologetic glances to the people around them.

"Gordon," she growled through gritted teeth, "this is ridiculous. Get up."

"I will when you give me your answer."

Teri saw Scott coming toward them with the manager right beside him.

"No. Gordon, the answer is no. Please get up!"

He rose, unruffled, with his eyes locked on hers. She felt as if, uninvited, this man were looking into the window of her soul. "I can wait," he said in a low steady voice.

Twenty-Five

❧

Teri stood at the airport baggage claim carousel in Eugene, Oregon, waiting for her lone suitcase to inch its way over to her. She lifted it with a huff and trudged out to the curb where Jessica had agreed to pick Teri up. As soon as she stepped out of the terminal, Teri spotted Kyle's truck. Kyle and Jessica were seated inside waving at her.

Kyle, Jessica's firefighter husband, hopped out of the driver's side and came over to Teri with his arms open. "Welcome home, Teri! Did you have a good time?"

"Don't ask," Teri muttered, handing him her suitcase, which he hoisted into the flat bed of his truck. She opened the passenger door, climbed in, and gave Jessica a hug.

Kyle got in, and they both looked at Teri.

"So," Jessica said, flipping her honey-blond hair over her shoulder, "how was your vacation?"

"Exhausting," Teri said. "I don't want to talk about it. I'd rather hear about your honeymoon. How was your cruise?"

"Wonderful," Kyle answered, gazing at Jessica with a newlywed's smitten look. Their wedding had been five weeks ago, two days before Teri had left for Maui. She had been one of Jessica's bridesmaids and had walked down the aisle of their little church in Glenbrooke with an armful of pink roses. The romantic wedding was beautiful and had flung Teri into a fantasy about Mark only days before she saw him. Funny how so much had changed in a little more than a month.

"I'm glad you had a good time," Teri said. "Maybe I'll have to try the Caribbean on my next vacation. I'm certainly never going back to Maui again!"

Kyle pulled into the flow of traffic and headed for Glenbrooke. "You know you want to tell us," he said. "What happened over there?"

Teri had been friends with Kyle for several years before Jessica had moved to town. More than once Kyle and Teri had benefitted from heart-to-heart, brother-sister-type conversations. Teri considered Jessica her best friend. She might as well spill her guts to these two.

"I'll start with the good news. My sister is pregnant, and so far everything has gone perfectly. The doctor told her she shouldn't have to worry about a miscarriage this time, and I think she's going to be fine. Danny's really excited and proud and all that."

"That's terrific," Jessica said. She sat in the middle between Teri and Kyle. Teri couldn't help but notice how close Jessica was sitting to Kyle, much closer than she needed to make room for Teri on the bench seat. It almost looked as if they were sewn together at the thigh. Teri wondered what it would be like to feel that close to a man. In a way, she was jealous that Jessica was experiencing something she was sure she never would, not after all she had just gone through.

"Now tell us the bad news," Kyle said. "I take it things didn't work out with you and…what was that guy's name?"

"Mark. No, things didn't work out with Mark. He's with a sweet woman named Claire, and I'm very happy for him."

"I'm sorry, Teri," Jessica said.

"Wait, there's more! I met a man who went to my high school and made a total fool of myself for several weeks trying to believe something lasting was going on between us. I completely deluded myself. We weren't right for each other at all. It was as if I were bent on proving something to myself or to my sister. She and I fought most of the time I was there, mostly over Scott, and I came close to leaving Glenbrooke and my life here to try a risky business venture with Scott and my brother-in-law. I was going to make tamales. Can you believe that?"

"Tamales sound good right about now. Are either of you hungry?" Kyle said.

"Kyle!" Jessica gently swatted his arm. "When a woman is sharing her heart with you, you don't ask if she's hungry."

"Sorry," he said with a good-natured shrug. "Go on, Teri. You were involved with a guy named Scott."

"We didn't really get involved. Well, I guess we did. My heart sure did. I think. I don't know. I'm so confused. I just need to be home and back to my regular life and forget this whole fiasco."

Graciously, Jessica changed the subject and started to tell Teri about their big project, restoring the old Victorian house at the top of Madison Hill. It had been boarded up for more than eight years. They had bought it, hired a team of workers, and planned to move in before Christmas. Now they were living in Kyle's house, which was a large, ranch-style home on the outskirts of town. Jessica had once said she didn't mind living there for awhile, but it was too rugged for her, with its timber beams running through the ceiling of the downstairs. The Victorian mansion was about as opposite to Kyle's house as Teri could imagine. But Kyle seemed enthusiastic about the project.

When they dropped Teri off at her little bungalow, Jessica said, "Would it be okay if I stopped by in a few days? I know you'll want to settle in and everything, but call me when you're ready for visitors."

Teri called her two days later. She had done enough soul searching, crying, and moping and was ready for some company. They planned to meet at noon, and Teri made up a salad for them. Jessica arrived with a basket of croissants from the bakery, and the two friends sat down in Teri's cozy kitchen, ready to pick up their friendship where they had left off. So much had happened to both of them during the past month and a half.

"So," Teri began, "tell me all about married life. Is it like you thought it would be?"

"I think so," Jessica said. She wasn't a beautiful woman, but she was lovely, with a simple, gentle appearance. Her reserved disposition had been a refreshing encouragement to Teri when they had first met since Teri tended to be direct and blunt in her approach to everything. Their friendship ran deep, and Teri felt she could trust Jessica with her heart. She hoped Jessica felt the same about her.

"In some ways I don't feel married," Jessica said. "I don't know how to explain it. It all feels natural to me, as if we were supposed to be together, and since we're married, of course we live together and eat together and sleep together." She broke off a corner of her croissant and looked thoughtful. "Teri, it's strange. What I feel for Kyle is so powerful, so intense. But in our everyday lives, it's just normal. I mean, it's wonderful to be, you know…united completely. But it's just normal like that's the way it should be. I'm not explaining this very well."

"I think I understand what you're saying. I sort of saw that with my sister and her husband."

"I guess I always thought of marriage as this huge mystery. You find the right person, and you become one, and somehow everything changes. Things don't really change. They go on, only now it's, I don't know…fuller. Deeper. Richer and more complete."

"You're kind of disappointing me here, Jess. I thought you would have all kinds of romantic stories to tell me of wild passion and endless fireworks."

Jessica smiled, and the scar on the top of her lip curled slightly. "Oh, believe me, there are fireworks." For a moment she seemed to float off.

"Well, that's comforting," Teri said.

Jessica cleared her throat. "That part of my marriage is between Kyle and me." A sweet smile lingered on her lips. "What I'm talking about is the day-to-day part of being with someone. It's funny how opposites attract. I never would have pictured myself with a man like Kyle. Now I can't picture myself with anyone but Kyle."

Teri thought of Mark and Scott. She couldn't see herself with either of them now. She had centered so much of her concern on the chemistry between her and "Mr. Right," and now Jessica was telling her the real power emerges from the ordinary, the day-to-day camaraderie. Strange. Her focus had turned to a quest for romance, and she had been drawn to two men whom she didn't even particularly enjoy being around.

"Jessica, I think I need to see a counselor. I am so messed up right now. I don't know what to look for in a relationship. Maybe I'm not supposed to be married. Maybe I'm one of those people who's better off single for the rest of her life. But then why did God give me these desires? I want to love a man with my entire being. I want children. Lots of children. I want to be married." Tears welled up in Teri's eyes and began to splash down her cheek. "I think it's me. I'm a loser."

Jessica calmly moved around the table and slipped her arm around Teri's shoulder. "You are *not* a loser," she said firmly. "Do you remember what you told me last fall when someone delivered those groceries to my door? I'll never forget it. You said, 'When we surrender to God, he works in awesome ways.' You told me that he supernaturally works everything out for the best. At the time, I wasn't even on speaking terms with God, but your words stuck with me."

Teri wiped her tears with her napkin. Inwardly she scolded herself for having passed out such easy answers to Jessica. She didn't mind Jessica tossing them back at her, almost a year later, but Teri had come to view life as a complex tangle of emotions and events. Easy answers didn't work for her anymore.

"Jess, I appreciate what you're trying to do here. I'm just finding that I'm a much more intense person than I realized, and I'm having a hard time figuring out what I'm doing wrong."

Jessica returned to her chair and after a few moments said, "Do you know Robert Burns?"

"Does he live in Glenbrooke?"

"No, Robert Burns the Scottish poet. I had to memorize some of his work in college, and one of his prayers just came to me. Would you mind if I quoted it to you?"

Teri shrugged, and Jessica plunged in.

> Thou knowest that Thou hast formed me
> With passions wild and strong;
> And listening to their witching voice
> Has often led me wrong.
>
> Where with intention I have erred,
> No other plea I have,
> But, Thou art good; and Goodness still
> Delighteth to forgive.

Teri tried to remember Jessica's quote after she left. She agreed that her passions were wild and strong indeed. And, as she thought about forgiveness, a long flow of prayers tumbled from her lips. "Father, I did err with my intentions, didn't I? I was so eager to love and be loved that I was willing to commit myself to Scott even though he barely knew you. I was looking on the outside. You look on the heart. Oh, God please forgive me. Cleanse me. Prepare me for the right man. A man who loves you and who wants to spend the rest of his life loving me."

It helped to pour out her heart in prayer. However, Teri couldn't help but feel her prayer for such a man was a bit of a dreamer's lark. It was hard to believe such a man existed on planet earth.

Twenty-Six

Within two weeks of Teri's return from Maui she was becoming her old self again. Life in Glenbrooke was pleasant, and her days were filled with good friends and lots of summer garage sales. The intense desire for a husband that had driven her to Maui seemed to be subsiding as she prepared for another year of teaching at Glenbrooke High School.

Anita had called the Sunday after Teri had returned to Oregon. Within the first five minutes of their conversation, Teri felt as if everything were peaceful between them. Annie mentioned briefly that Dan was thinking about taking some correspondence courses in business. As a result of the tamale idea, Dan had discovered he had more of a head for business than he had realized. Annie saw it as something good that had come out of the whole tamale thing, and she thanked Teri for allowing Dan to drag her through such extensive plans, even though it was a far-fetched idea. Teri was comforted to know Dan wasn't mad at her for backing out.

On the fourth Sunday after she had returned, it was Teri's turn to call Annie. She decided the time had come to ask about Scott.

"Scott?" Annie said in a teasing voice. "Who's Scott?"

"Come on, Anita. Don't be like that. Have you seen him or talked to him?"

"Not since the day you left when he came over here and tried to talk you out of your decision to dump him."

"I didn't dump him," Teri said, silently remembering how strained that conversation had been. Scott had showed up at the front door right after she had climbed out of the shower. Her hair was dripping wet, and she stood in the living room, wrapped up in Dan's robe that had been hanging on the bathroom door. Scott had said he wanted to know if he could say or do anything to change her mind. She told him it had become clear to her that they were each in search of two completely different relationships. She was looking for a relationship that would lead to marriage. Scott had said, "I'm not the kind who can make a lifelong commitment like that. Why can't you be willing to take it as it comes?"

Teri had used his phrase back on him. "Because I guess I'm not the kind who can take it as it comes. I need a lifelong commitment."

Scott had looked deep into her eyes and said, "So for you, it's marriage or nothing."

Teri nodded.

"Too bad," Scott said, running his finger along her cheek and grasping a handful of her curls one last time. "We'll never know how good we could have been together." And then he had left.

Teri shook the memory from her mind and spoke into the receiver. "Scott and I agreed it wasn't working out. It wasn't meant to be. I didn't dump him."

"You don't have to try to convince me that you two weren't

meant to be," Annie said. "I never thought it would work out. I just wish you hadn't gone through so much grief coming to the same conclusion."

"Yes, all-wise and all-knowing sister, I know, I know. I guess I kind of hoped against hope that maybe Scott had started going to church on his own or something."

"Nope. Oh, but Gordon sends his love."

Teri felt a funny, warm sensation at Annie's words. Even though Gordon was peculiar, he was one of the kinder, friendlier memories of her vacation. She never had told Annie or anyone else about Gordon's ridiculous gesture at Kimo's. She had written his comical proposal off to Gordon being on Annie and Dan's side when it came to opinions about Scott. When Gordon heard Scott's comments about not planning to marry her and wanting to just live with her, Gordon obviously had tried to sidetrack Teri's attention and get her mind off Scott. He probably had thought his antics worked since Teri and Scott broke up. But she had made that decision before Gordon spilled the tea.

She hadn't seen Gordon again before she left the islands. If she had, she probably would have patted him on the back and thanked him for his last ditch effort to divert her from Scott Robinson, even though it was unnecessary.

"How is the ol' Gordo?" Teri asked.

"He leaves tomorrow to go back to seminary on the mainland. He preached this morning, and Teri, you should have been there. That man has the hand of God on him."

"It's probably a good thing," Teri said. "Otherwise he would be tripping all over the place."

"That's not nice! You know he has an equilibrium problem, don't you?"

"Yes, I know very well." She proceeded to tell Anita about the incident on the rocks that had brought Teri tumbling into the ocean.

"I didn't know that! Why didn't you tell me when you were here?"

"I didn't tell you a lot of things, Annie, and I regret that now. I wish I had the whole summer to do over again. I'm glad I went through everything I did, but I wish I could have figured out all this relationship stuff in high school, like most people do. I was not at my best this summer."

"Yeah, well I was no picnic to be around, and I'm sorry for that. I'm starting to feel better now that I'm in my second trimester. My system and my hormones seem to be balancing out a little better. At least that's what Dan says."

"And the doctor? What does he have to say?"

"I don't go again for two more weeks, but so far everything is great. With the other two babies I didn't make it this far into the pregnancy, so I'm feeling pretty good about that, too. It's been a day-by-day, step-of-faith time for me."

"You know, even though this summer was not at all how I thought it would be, I'm still glad I was able to be there when you found out you were pregnant."

"I'm glad you were here, too. When are you coming back?"

"Oh…maybe never."

Annie laughed. "Come on, you have to come see your niece."

"Your nephew," Dan shouted in the background.

"Did you hear that?" Anita said.

"Yes. Tell Dan he's outnumbered two to one in favor of a girl."

"I'll tell him. I have to get going. I'll send you a tape of Gordon's sermon from this morning."

The tape came a week and a half later, and Teri put it on the bookshelf in her bedroom where it collected dust for weeks. The school year was off to a promising start, and Teri was caught up in all the activity. Glenbrooke High's principal, Mr. McGregor, returned after suffering a stroke the year before, which had kept him out the entire school year. The interim principal, Charlotte Mendelson, had run off the last week of school with the football coach. For this small town, it had been a major scandal. Many of the parents were concerned about what kind of school year they could expect in the fall. But with the return of Hugh McGregor, the whole community seemed to breathe easier and parental involvement was at an all-time high.

Teri's schedule consisted of three beginning Spanish classes made up mostly of freshmen. She had two intermediate classes, which were a mix of grade levels, and then her favorite, the advanced class of fourteen bright seniors, fell on her last period of the day.

As she had for the past three years, Teri helped out with the high school group at church. Many of the students were in her classes, which meant she had a close rapport with them.

Kyle was the volunteer youth director at their church, and Jessica was involved right beside him. She taught high school English, and her classroom was next to Teri's.

Everything seemed normal, steady, busy, fulfilling. No new and interesting men had moved to Glenbrooke. None of the old, familiar single guys took up an interest in Teri. It was the same old situation. Yet she settled into her routine, feeling moderately content and fully herself.

Only when her life was back in full swing did she realize how crazy the summer had been. Never again would she allow herself to go through such a personality transformation in a quest for a spouse. If God wanted her to be married, she decided that he would have to do it, as Jessica had reminded her, in a supernatural way.

The second week of December, Teri finally gave in to a cold that had been pestering her since Thanksgiving. She called in sick on Tuesday and spent the day in bed. The next morning she woke to find that her voice was gone. It made it tricky to call in sick. She whispered her message into the answering machine at 7:30 and hoped the secretary would be able to decode it. The laryngitis lasted three long and boring days.

On Friday afternoon she came across the tape of Gordon's sermon, popped it into her Walkman, and went about her chosen therapy of making a huge batch of tamales. It was the first time she had embarked on the lengthy project since Maui, and she felt melancholy.

Then she switched on the tape, and Gordon's smooth voice with its charming accent filled her ears and ran right through her. She had never heard anyone preach with such clarity and compassion. It was as if he were speaking to one person, sharing his heart openly and unashamedly. At the center of his heart was his clear love for God.

The approach was completely different from her father's. Her dad preached loud, with powerful words and grand hand gestures.

She enjoyed Gordon's message so much that she listened to it twice and rewound it at the end to catch the final few lines of his unique benediction again.

"Until," Gordon said. "Until that day. And may we live today as if tomorrow were that day."

She had heard him say his "until" salutation more than once but had never imagined what he meant by it. Now she thought his reference to "that day" might mean the day a believer dies and goes to be with the Lord. Or maybe he meant the day that Jesus returns. At any rate, the thought was intriguing, living today as if tomorrow one would stand face-to-face with Jesus.

By six o'clock that evening the tamales were completed, and the kitchen was a disaster. The doorbell rang. Kyle stood there with a pizza box in his hands. Jessica was beside him, holding a grocery bag.

"Did you know," Kyle said in a deep voice, "that the best cure for laryngitis is an extra large with pepperoni?"

Teri smiled at her buddies and welcomed them inside.

"Smells like you already have dinner going," Kyle said, whiffing the air like Smoky the Bear. "And if you don't mind my saying, it smells better than what we brought you."

Teri pulled a large Ziploc bag full of tamales from the refrigerator and handed them to Kyle with a big smile.

"Oh, no, Teri, I was only kidding. I don't want to take your tamales."

She opened the refrigerator and freezer at the same time, exposing her blow-out supply of tamales. "Did you make all these?" Jessica asked, looking stunned. She wasn't much of a cook, having grown up with servants and chefs.

Teri nodded and gestured that Kyle should take the tamales and warm them up in the steamer on the stove.

"Well, if you insist," Kyle said. "Maybe just one. Or two."

"Or the whole bag," Jessica teased. Turning to Teri she said, "You've just made my husband a very happy man. The only thing I've successfully prepared for him so far is Marie Callender's frozen lasagna, which I cooked in the microwave."

"Now, Jess, that's not true. One night you made that really good meat loaf."

"I hate to break it to you, honey. That one came from a Marie Callender box too."

"Man, do these smell good," Kyle said, going about his tamale preparation with gusto. "You should sell these, Teri. You could make a fortune!"

Teri rolled her eyes while Jessica filled in the words for her. "Don't you remember, Kyle? That's what she was thinking about doing on Maui. The guy she was dating and her brother-in-law were going to set her up in business."

"Oh, yeah," Kyle said.

"He doesn't remember," Jessica said to Teri on the side.

Teri motioned with her hand that it didn't matter. She pulled some plates from the cupboard. She had thirty-two plates in her cupboard, all fine china, from garage sales. Only two of them matched, which was her decorating scheme. Most of her house was done in simple ivory colors. The walls, the counters, and floors were all off-white. Even her couch was a sandy beige. But her accessories were a bright patchwork of colors. She had fabric covers on her kitchen chairs, each chair a different fabric. Her couch was lined with pillows in a zoo of shapes and colors. Throughout her house were lively pockets of color and design.

Some people were bothered by it, saying it didn't follow a set pattern. Teri didn't care. It was she.

In every way her life matched her home: the basic pattern was there, but the details were less predictable.

She reached for some glasses and was about to fill them with water when Jessica opened the grocery bag. "I brought some Snapple," she said. "And of course," she reached her hand into the bottom of the bag and produced a box of DoveBars, "the essential ingredient for any successful dinner party. I just thought of something, though. How are we going to fit these into that packed freezer?" Jessica tore open the box.

"Oh, you guys, they're starting to melt. I guess we'll have to eat our dessert first. Here, Teri." Jessica handed Teri one of the ice cream bars and another one to Kyle. "Cheers!" They all laughed and "toasted" with their DoveBars.

Teri chomped into her bar and thought how blessed she was to have friends like Kyle and Jessica. She would have missed both of them if she had moved to Maui.

Just then the phone rang. Teri attempted to answer it. Her "hello" came out froggy.

"Is Teri there?"

"This is Teri."

Her voice sounded so deep and raspy that the person asked again. "Is Teri Moreno there?"

"It's me," she barked. "I have laryngitis."

"Oh, Teri, you sound awful. It's Lauren. I hope I'm not bothering you."

Teri hadn't heard from her old college roommate in months. They kept in contact only through occasional phone calls and Christmas and birthday cards. Teri gestured to Kyle and Jessica to excuse her and took the phone into the living room.

"How are you?" Teri rasped out.

"Well, actually," Laurel said slowly, "I'm doing quite well."

"Good!"

"I received your Christmas card," Laurel continued. "And I realized I hadn't talked to you in a long time so you didn't know what was happening in my life. I was going to write you, but then I thought it would be easier if I called."

"Let me guess," Teri whispered. "You've moved up the wedding date."

Lauren and Jeff had been engaged since Easter. They had been dating for almost a year, ever since Lauren had returned to her hometown in Tennessee. She had graduated from college two years after Teri, then spent a year trying to find a permanent job in California. Finally Lauren had given up and gone home. That's when she had met Jeff. He was the best thing that had happened to her in a long time.

Lauren paused before saying, "Actually, Jeff and I broke up. I know I should have told you sooner, but I didn't realize until I received your Christmas card that you didn't know."

"Oh, Lauren, I'm sorry!" Teri finally said.

"I am, too," Lauren said in a whisper laced with much pain.

Twenty-Seven

By the time Teri finished her conversation with Lauren, she felt exhausted. Her throat throbbed from straining it.

"I'm sorry," Teri whispered to Jessica and Kyle as she walked back into the kitchen. They were standing by the sink, their dinners already finished and their dirty plates on the counter. And they were wrapped up in a tender embrace with their eyes closed. They didn't notice that Teri had entered. It was a beautiful sight after what she had just heard on the phone.

Teri tapped a bottle of Snapple on the counter, and Jessica jumped and pulled away, slightly blushing. Kyle smiled as if he had nothing to be embarrassed about and kept his arm around Jessica's shoulder.

"I'm sorry. That was my college roommate," Teri explained hoarsely." She was calling to tell me her engagement is broken."

"Is she going to be okay?" Jessica asked.

"She sounded like it. Lauren is a strong person."

"Where does she live?" Kyle asked.

"Tennessee."

"Do you think you should go be with her?" Jessica said. "I know that's kind of far, but…"

"Does she need to get away?" Kyle asked. "She could come here. There's plenty of room at our house, and when we move out next week, she could stay there as long as she needed to."

Teri shrugged, trying to use her facial expressions to convey her appreciation and save her voice. "I don't know what she's going to do. She didn't seem to have her next step figured out yet. She has a job at a bank, but that's not what she really wants to do. She was an art major in college."

"We're serious," Kyle said. "Any way we can help out, just holler."

"Thanks for bringing the pizza," Teri said.

"Hey, it's all yours. We gorged on tamales. I'm telling you, Teri, they're the best I've ever had. Thanks."

"Are you ready for some pizza?" Jessica asked.

She shook her head.

"We'll squeeze it into the fridge then," Jessica said. "It'll make a good midnight snack."

"We need to get going," Kyle said. "Is there anything we can bring you tomorrow? Some tea or something for your throat?"

Teri shook her head. Even though she sounded awful, she didn't feel very sick, just shaken by Lauren's call. She took another bag of tamales from the refrigerator and handed them to Kyle.

"Oh, I couldn't."

Teri pushed them at him.

"Well, if you insist."

"Let us know if we can help you or Lauren in any way, okay?" Jessica asked, reaching for her purse on the counter. It amazed

Teri how down to earth Jessica was. One would never guess by looking at the woman, by the way she dressed or how she carried herself, that she was worth double-digit millions. She never let it show, but she was one of the most generous people Teri had ever known. Kyle was the same way. Neither of them were flashy in how they gave. They helped in quiet, practical ways, such as offering to pick her up at the airport when she came home from Maui, bringing over dinner, or offering Lauren a place to stay. Teri saw them to the door and waved her thanks as they walked to the truck with their arms around each other.

What a contrast! Teri thought. *Two people intensely in love and two other people across the country who just called off their engagement. Would I have ended up like Lauren if I had stayed with Scott?*

The night was a restless one for Teri. She woke up around two o'clock, perspiring and fitful. Her initial waking thought was that someone had died. Then she remembered it wasn't a death, but Lauren's call that had swept her emotions to the edge of this jagged precipice. Teri padded into the kitchen for a drink of water and made a face at the mountain of dirty dishes still stacked in the sink. She went into the living room and curled up on the couch with all her pillows.

In a way, it almost was news of a death. Certainly a fateful blow had been dealt to her friend's heart. How could a man break a promise like that?

For almost an hour, Teri fought an invisible war, trying to figure out what had gone wrong with Lauren and Jeff. He had definitely swept Lauren off her feet in one easy swoop. For a while the previous spring, Lauren had called often with details of their wedding plans. She had sent clippings from *Bride's* magazine, so Teri could see the wedding dress and bridesmaids' dresses. The wedding had been scheduled for April, on the one-year anniversary of their engagement. They seemed to have done everything right, and yet it had all fallen apart.

Lauren hadn't gone into a lot of details on the phone. She had sounded as if she were handling it well. Still, it must have broken her heart.

Teri went back to bed. In the hazy tunnel of her mind, between sleeping and waking, she prayed for her friend. And she wondered if what had happened to Lauren might not happen to her one day. Couldn't she find herself in a similar situation: feeling sure she had made the right choice in a mate and yet, even while she was caught up in her wedding plans, ending up watching all her dreams disintegrate?

When she woke the next morning, Teri felt more than a little shaken. No relationship was guaranteed. She was better off for having ended her relationship with Scott—or with any man, for that matter. Teri felt the only safe place to be was alone, single for the rest of her life. It was the only sure answer, the only guarantee she wouldn't be crushed later in life.

With the devastation of Lauren's engagement came the ruin of a dream for Teri, a dream of marriage and children of her own. She couldn't, *wouldn't* let her heart be smashed like that.

She didn't say anything or make any outward adjustments to her life. But inside her heart, written on stone tablets, were the words: Thou shalt not fall in love. Thou shalt not get married. Thou shalt not have children.

Twenty-Eight

Teri's voice returned just in time for her to complete her last week of teaching before Christmas vacation. She helped Jessica and Kyle move into their new home in the evenings and did her Christmas shopping by catalog over the phone during her lunch breaks.

Teri planned to go home to Escondido for Christmas. Her flight left on Sunday afternoon, which meant she had a day and a half to organize everything after her last day of teaching. She went over to Kyle and Jessica's new house on Saturday morning with her gift of several bags of tamales. Kyle was especially appreciative. Their new home was beautiful.

"It looks as if you guys are all set here," Teri said, scanning the living room with its ornate marble fireplace and exquisite wooden mantle. The furniture and walls weren't overdone, but they were definitely Victorian and fit the style of the house beautifully.

"All we need is a couple of hydrangea bushes out front, and it's home," Kyle said. He shot a look at Jessica, and she returned the loving expression with a lingering intimacy. Teri noticed that they seemed to draw strength from each other.

"Oh," Jessica said, slowly looking away from Kyle and going over to the oak rolltop desk, "I have something for you, Teri." She handed her an envelope and said, "I know it's not fancy, but I didn't have a chance to wrap it. Go ahead and open it."

Teri slit the envelope and pulled out what looked like an airplane ticket. "What's this?"

"It's good for any time and any destination. You just call that number and tell them where you want to go and when. I thought you might want to use it when Anita's baby comes. Or maybe you could go see Lauren in Tennessee. I know it's kind of a weird gift, but I wanted to buy you something you could use."

Teri hugged her. "This is so sweet of you! Thanks, Jess."

"You're welcome. And thank you for feeding us for the next week with your tamales!"

"You think they'll last that long?" Kyle asked.

Jessica smiled and said, "Okay, make that for the next two hours."

"When do you leave?" Kyle asked.

"Tomorrow afternoon."

"Do you want a ride to the airport?"

"No, I decided to drive and leave my car at the airport. I'll only be gone five days. Thanks, anyway." Teri slipped the envelope into her purse and hugged her friends good-bye. "Have a wonderful Christmas! I need to get going. I have eight more tamale deliveries, and I need to pack."

"Be sure to thank your mom for teaching you the art of tamale making," Kyle called out as she left. "Tell her we appreciate it more than she'll ever know."

Teri remembered his words several days later when she was seated at the family dining table, enjoying her mom's enchiladas. Her mom passed the credit onto her mother, who was seated next to Teri.

Grandma Maria leaned over and tapped Teri on the hand. She said, "You have learned what you need to make your *esposo* happy—good cooking."

"Now all she needs is an *esposo,*" one of her brothers said.

I don't need a husband! Teri couldn't bring herself to voice her feelings and decided it would be better to endure the string of comments that were sure to follow about her being the oldest of all her sisters and cousins who weren't married.

It hurt. She tried to ignore it, but as the holidays unfolded, she realized that in her family she was a loner. On Christmas Day seventeen people were crammed into her parents' living room. She noticed that everybody had somebody—everybody but her. Even her fourteen-year-old sister, the baby of the family, had received a heart-shaped necklace the day before from a guy at school who liked her.

Teri tried to convince herself that she could be single and still be important to this family. Her Aunt Yolanda was. She had forged her way into the business world and was now at the executive level. However, Teri didn't have those kinds of ambitions.

One of her cousins handed Teri her four-month-old baby boy so she could help her two-year-old son open his gifts. Teri watched the big family merriment and the flurry of unwrapped gifts, all accompanied with happy squeals. She rocked the little one, and he fell asleep in her arms.

She felt a deep sadness, but she kept it to herself. For the most part, Teri enjoyed her family and the Christmas fun. It was a lively yet sacred time for her family, and she was glad to be with them all. If only she didn't feel so alone and fated to be alone forever.

On the morning after Christmas, the telephone rang at 5:00 A.M., waking Teri, who was sleeping on the couch. Her mom answered the phone in the bedroom and a few minutes later came hurrying down the hallway.

Teri met her mom in the kitchen. "Who called?"

Her mom looked dazed and a little frightened. "It was Danny. They're at the hospital. The baby is coming!"

"Are you sure, Mom? She's not due for another two months."

"Oh, Teri," her mom said, grasping her hands, "we must pray."

As the two women began to pray, Teri's dad joined them in the kitchen and entered into their prayers. Before they were finished, four other family members, including Grandma Maria, had joined them in the praying.

When the last amen was said, Teri's mom set about making coffee.

"Mom," Teri said, sliding up behind her and giving her a comforting hug, "why don't you go be with Annie? I have a ticket you can use. It's good for any time."

"No, I couldn't use your ticket."

Teri's father overheard and entered the discussion, agreeing with Teri that Mom should go, but they could buy a ticket for her. Then Grandma Maria thought she should go, too. When all the discussion ended, it was agreed that Teri, Mom, and Grandma would all travel to Hawaii as soon as possible.

Teri retreated to the bedroom phone and called the airline. She made arrangements for the three of them to leave that morning. A frantic scramble ensued, and nearly ten hours later the three Moreno women stood together on Hawaiian soil.

"You did tell Dan what flight we were on, didn't you?" Mom asked, with the worry lines deepening in her face.

"Yes, of course I did," Teri assured her. "He wasn't going to leave the hospital, so he said he would send a friend to pick us up."

They stood together at the baggage claim, all three of them still in shock over how quickly everything was happening. No one approached them, saying he was Danny's friend who had come to retrieve them.

As soon as they had all their bags together, Teri said, "Look, you two stay here, and I'll make a couple of phone calls. I should have told him we would rent a car. We can still do that."

Teri was surprised the airport was so much more crowded than it had been that summer. Maui appeared to be a favorite vacation spot for Christmas. She couldn't blame any of these people for wanting to be here.

The minute she had stepped off the plane and the warm island breezes had greeted her, she had remembered how deeply she loved this island and how she had wanted to move here long before anyone had thought up the tamale business and long before she had run into Scott. Once again the desire rose within her, and she wished she were moving here, not just visiting, especially under such panicky circumstances.

She headed for the phone but stopped when she saw a familiar face. Renegade strands of brown hair swept across the face, while laugh lines stretched from the corners of his blue eyes. The fit Australian waved at Teri and jogged toward her.

Look out for that trash can, Gordon!

He maneuvered past it with only a pinch to spare.

"It's a girl!" he shouted breathlessly. "Only three pounds, but she's alive."

Teri felt an impulse to hug him, but with the shot of adrenalin his words brought, she turned and hustled back to her mom and grandmother, shouting as soon as she saw them. Gordon followed on her heels.

"How do you know this?" Grandma asked, looking confused.

Teri introduced Gordon and let him relay the whole story to the three of them. The baby was born a little more than an hour ago, and Annie was doing fine. They wouldn't know much more until the doctors had completed their exam.

Gordon took the luggage from the hands of the older women and showed them to his car in the parking lot. They drove straight to the hospital.

Only two people could go in to see Anita at a time, the nurse insisted. Mom and Grandma scooted right in while Danny took a break and went to find something to eat. Teri, who had located a couch in a corner room down the hall, collapsed on it.

Not until her spinning mind started to slow down did it sink in to Teri that Gordon was sitting beside her. He must have been there a full five minutes, quietly leafing through a magazine, not speaking, not pushing in any way, just being there with her.

"Thanks for picking us up, Gordon." Teri smiled at him. He returned the smile, and Teri felt as if something inside her had started to come back to life, like dying embers in a fire that had been fanned back to a red glow. She realized she hadn't seen Gordon or talked to him since that night at Kimos last summer. Yet she felt comfortable sitting there with him. It seemed natural for him to be involved in a family crisis. Perhaps it was his pastoral position.

"Teri," Gordon began to say something and then stopped. He looked at her intently, as if his serious blue eyes were peering through a window into her soul.

What do you see? she thought. *How can you connect yourself to me like that, so instantly and uninvited?* It occurred to Teri that she felt she had nothing to hide from this man. They were somehow united. Whether it was over this emergency or a result of their long and honest talks in the crater, she wasn't sure. But at this moment, Teri felt as if the real her had somehow become intimately connected to this man, and she had done nothing to initiate such a connection.

"Teri," he said again, tilting his good ear toward her, "I..."

Before Gordon could get out his words, Teri's grandma stepped into the room and said, "Teresa, it's your turn."

It took Teri a moment to break away from her eye contact with Gordon. "All right," she said, slowly looking up at her grandmother. "How's she doing?"

Grandma Maria didn't answer. She looked at Teri with an expression of delightful surprise and then at Gordon as if she had noticed him for the first time. Grandma mumbled an exclamation of amazement to herself in Spanish. As Teri rose, Grandma sat down next to Gordon and, patting his hand, said, "So, now, tell me all about yourself."

Twenty-Nine

❧

Hi," Teri said, gently sitting on the edge of Annie's bed. "We were right, weren't we? It's a girl."

Mom stood at the head of the bed, tenderly brushing Annie's hair off her forehead.

"Oh, Teri, she's so tiny," Anita said. "So tiny. I don't see how—"

"Shh," Mom interrupted. "Don't speak, *mi hija*. It's in God's hands. Shh."

After a few moments of awkward silence, Teri asked, "How are you feeling?"

"Okay. I'm glad you're all here. You didn't have to do this, you know."

"Oh, yes we did. The Moreno women stick together when it really matters. And you really matter to all of us, Annie," Teri said.

"I told Mom I've been waiting for years to have her come visit me. If this is what I have to do to get her here, I'm not sure I want to guarantee many more visits."

Teri smiled. Anita didn't look right. Perhaps it was the

exhaustion of childbirth or the nervous fatigue over not knowing what was going to happen to the baby.

"Have you decided on a name for her?"

Anita shook her head. "We weren't ready for her yet. I don't even have a crib or anything. I planned to use the money we received yesterday for Christmas gifts from everyone." She wrinkled her forehead. "Was Christmas yesterday or the day before?"

"It was yesterday," Mom said. "You need some rest, Annie. Then I'm sure you'll feel better."

"I want to wait until the doctor comes back. I won't be able to sleep until I hear what he has to say."

"Why don't you try just to rest," Teri suggested. "We'll be right here, and I promise we'll wake you up the second he walks in that door."

Then, as if Teri's words had been the doctor's cue, the door opened, and an older man with white hair and a matching white coat stepped in. "Well!" he said, seeming surprised to see Teri and her mom. "Visitors already?" He extended a handshake to both of them. "Dr. Vaughan," he said as a simple introduction.

"This is my mom and sister." Anita's voice pitched a little higher than usual. "They just arrived from the mainland."

"West Coast, I take it," he said, looking at them over the top of his half-glasses. He seemed easygoing and friendly. Teri couldn't tell if the chart in his hand bore good news or devastation for Anita.

"Southern California," Mom answered. "Would you like us to go find Danny?"

"No, I just spoke with him in the hallway. He said he would join us in a minute."

Teri moved so Dr. Vaughan could be by Anita's side.

"They don't have to leave, do they?" Anita asked.

"It's up to you," he said.

"I'd like them to stay." Anita reached up and took hold of her mother's hand, waiting for the report on her baby girl.

"Okay, well then," Dr. Vaughan took Teri's flattened space on the edge of the bed and opened his chart. "Let me go through everything with you. First, your daughter weighed in at three pounds and fifteen ounces."

Teri cringed. She saw Mom and Annie squeeze hands.

"Her heart is quite strong, her lungs not fully developed. But we didn't find any obvious problems with them. She's not yet able to breathe on her own, so she'll be on oxygen for some time."

"How long?" Anita asked.

"It's hard to say at this point. We'll know better in about a week. Our main concern now is keeping her weight stable and protecting her from any infections. She's in isolation, but of course you and Dan can be with her whenever you want. Did I leave anything out?" He scanned the chart.

"Are her chances very good?" Anita wanted to know. "I mean, do you think she'll live?"

"Well, of course, we can never make any kind of guarantees in these matters," Dr. Vaughan said calmly. "But I'd say her chances are strong. Six months ago we had one here who weighed two pounds five ounces at birth and had a hole in his heart. We flew him to Honolulu, and he was actually home within three or four weeks. I saw him yesterday. Strong and healthy as can be. Your little girl is almost four pounds. That's a lot by today's medical standards."

Anita looked only slightly comforted. Teri felt for her. At least the baby was alive. At least she didn't have any major complications. There was a lot to be thankful for.

"Can we see her?" Teri's mom asked.

"Through the nursery window, yes. We're obviously trying to keep her away from as much contact with germs as possible." The doctor rose and gave Anita a warm smile. "She's really a beauty, you know. I think she has your looks."

Teri saw tears glistening in her sister's eyes.

"Now, I want to keep you here at least two more days, Anita. I'd like to see your blood pressure stabilized before we send you home."

"I don't mind being closer to my baby," Annie said.

Teri slipped out into the hallway and found Danny in the waiting room with Gordon and Grandma, finishing a sandwich.

"Is the doctor in the room now?" Dan asked, swallowing a bite.

"Yes. He gave us the update already. I guess you and Anita can see her whenever you're ready. Annie's looking awfully tired. I'm not sure it's helping that we're here."

"It's helping," Dan said, tossing the sandwich wrapper into the trash and chugging down a swig of his soft drink. "We're both glad you came."

They discussed their next step and decided it would be best if Teri, Mom, and Grandma left with Gordon and went to Dan and Annie's house. The hospital was nearly an hour's drive from their home, and it was already growing dark out. They couldn't do anything else at the hospital, and a good night's sleep would prepare them for the next few days of long hospital vigils ahead.

The trip seemed to be the hardest on Grandma Maria. It had all hit her so fast. She was confused for the first two days, but then her body seemed to fall into rhythm, and she forged ahead like a trooper. The women took turns at the hospital and spent many hours sitting with Dan and Anita.

Even though they looked through the glass window dozens of times at the little one in the clear plastic bassinet, they couldn't see her clearly.

Gordon came with them every day. Sometimes he would drive them over to the hospital and drop them off for the day. He would always call in or come by in the evening and drive them home. It seemed he was giving Grandma Maria rides more than anyone else. Teri and her mom preferred to stay as long as they could and ride home with Dan. They all fell into a pattern, their emotions rising or falling with each new bit of progress or regression.

The first two days the baby lost five ounces, which seemed a huge amount when she had been so little to start with. Anita was able to nurse the baby, which was good, and when her milk came in, the tiny little one gained one whole ounce that day. She gained two more ounces the next day, but on the fifth day she began to run a fever and wasn't even back to her birth weight yet.

Anita came home on the afternoon of the third day but only to sleep a few hours each night. Dan needed to get back to work, and although he swapped a few hours with some of the other guys, he still needed to work at least twenty hours.

A week went by, a week of blurred emotional ups and downs. They all slept at the house, at least from about midnight to six every day. Then they would rouse themselves and take the hour drive back to the hospital where Teri, her mom, and grandmother spent the day in front of the nursery window and in the waiting room.

It seemed there was nothing they could do. The baby appeared to be stabilizing, but who could tell? Anita was an emotional wreck, which is what prompted Teri to decide she would stay a little longer. Her mom and grandma had return tickets for January third, and it made sense for them to go on home.

The decision was hard, especially for Teri because she had already used up her sick leave. It meant she would have to request a leave of absence from her job.

She talked to Jessica about it at length one evening on the phone in the waiting room. Jessica encouraged her, saying she was doing the right thing.

"Even if you came back now," Jessica said, "I think your heart would be so attached to what's going on there that you wouldn't be at your best in the classroom. Besides, I think in a strange way it would be a blessing for Marita. She really needs the hours."

Marita was the substitute they called in for Teri in December when she was out with laryngitis. Marita lived in a little town about twenty miles from Glenbrooke and often substituted at Glenbrooke High School. Her area of specialty was Spanish, and since Teri was the only high school Spanish teacher within a fifty-mile radius, Marita didn't often get to do what she loved best.

"I guess you're right," Teri said. "At least I feel as if I'm leaving my class in good hands."

"You need to stay," Jessica said. "We'll continue to pick up your mail. I have a box of it here already. Why don't I just send it on to you? There's nothing pressing that you have to return for. Just stay, okay?"

"Okay," Teri agreed. "Do you have Mr. McGregor's phone number?"

"Why don't I make those calls for you?" Jessica suggested. "I can do it a lot easier from here. I'll call you back in a couple of days and let you know how everything turns out, okay?"

"Thanks, Jess. Did I ever tell you that you're one in a million?" The minute the words were out of her mouth, Teri wished she could suck them back in. Jessica hated any reference to her money. Teri hadn't meant it that way, and she hoped Jessica didn't read flippancy into the remark. Before Jessica could respond, Teri said, "My neighbor has a key to my house. Why don't you tell Kyle to pick it up and make good use of some of those tamales in my refrigerator? The ones in the freezer are okay, but the ones in the fridge should be eaten. Maybe he can treat the guys down at the station."

"Great idea," Jessica said. "By the way, have you seen Scott since you've been there?"

"No. I haven't even asked about him. It's been such a crazy schedule."

"I hope you don't mind my asking about him."

"No, of course not. It is kind of funny, though. I haven't thought of him more than two or three times since I've been here. And I don't feel anything for him. Is that normal?"

"Don't ask me! It's probably a sign that everything is resolved between you so you don't feel loose strings are hanging."

"I hope you're right," Teri said. Gordon walked into the waiting room just then and gave Teri his familiar little half wink. "I better go, Jess. Gordon's here."

"Gordon?" Jessica repeated. "The one who proposed to you at the restaurant that one night?"

226

Teri felt her cheeks begin to blush. She hadn't remembered that she had recounted that incident to Jessica. "Yes," she said in an even tone.

"Has he been around a lot?"

"Yes," Teri said again, not wanting to let on to Gordon that she was talking about him.

"Are you seeing Gordon with new eyes yet?"

Teri didn't answer. What was Jessica talking about? Was she trying to tease Teri because of the proposal incident?

"I'll talk to you in a couple of days," Teri said. "Thanks for making those calls for me."

"No problem. I'll talk to you later, and you can fill me in on all the details. Bye." Jessica hung up first.

Teri returned the phone to the corner of the table and turned to Gordon. He sat down next to her but seemed to have misjudged the distance because he ended up close to her. She guessed it must be his balance problem.

"I saw Dan. He said they finally named her. Did you hear?"

"Yes, Grace Malia. My grandma likes that they gave her the Hawaiian version of Maria for her middle name," Teri said. "Or did she already tell you that?"

"She did," Gordon said with a smile. "She also told me that you share her middle names: Angelina Raquel." His smile broadened, and he repeated Teri's full name as if it were a poem he had memorized, "Teresa Angelina Raquel Moreno." To him it was no longer unlisted.

Thirty

❦

I t's a mouthful, isn't it?" Teri said dryly. "And what's your middle name?"

"Thomas. Gordon Thomas Allister. Has a certain ring to it, don't you think?"

"Yes, it's very nice," Teri said. It seemed odd to her that his name didn't bother her the way it had when she first heard people calling him "Gordo." She always called him Gordon, and it now seemed to carry a certain dignity to it.

"Besides your middle name, your grandmother also told me she's planning to leave tomorrow with your mother. Are you going too?" His eyes looked into hers.

Teri looked away. She wasn't prepared for him to see into her soul as he had before. She gathered up her purse and address book from the table and said, "No, I've decided to stay awhile longer. A friend of mine is going to make the arrangements for a long-term sub for my classroom."

"Jessica?" Gordon asked.

Teri glanced at him. "Yes, how do you know about Jessica?"

"You've mentioned her before. Seems like a good friend of yours."

"Yes, she is. Well, I suppose we should tell Anita we're ready to go. I think she said she was going to stay here until Dan came after work." Teri and Gordon walked down the hall to the nursery. Mom and Grandma were standing at the window talking. They motioned to Anita through the glass that they were about to leave. Anita was dressed in a sterile gown, gloves, and hat and stood in the corner talking to one of the nurses. She waved goodbye and blew them a kiss.

Gordon offered Grandma his arm, as Teri had often seen him do, and they headed for the car. Grandma loved the attention. It seemed she loved Gordon, too, because she raved about him constantly. "He's such a fine man. So considerate. So selfless in his love for others. Mark my words; the hand of God is on that man."

Teri overheard him asking Grandma if she had ever smelled a tuberose before. He said he had something in the car for her. She chortled and squeezed his arm like a school girl. His words reminded Teri of how Gordon had bought the lei for her in the restaurant. That was a tuberose lei. She loved the fragrance from those flowers.

When Gordon opened his car door, that wonderful sweet fragrance met her nostrils again. He had three tuberose leis, one for each of them. He looped the first one over Grandma's fuzzy white hair and gave her a kiss on the cheek. Grandma kissed him right back on both his cheeks. Then he placed a lei around Mom's neck and offered her a kiss on the cheek.

Teri stood waiting for hers and felt her heart beating. *Is he going to kiss me, too?* She knew it was the island's custom and not at all unusual, but for some reason the sudden anticipation of being kissed on the cheek by Gordon Thomas Allister gave her butterflies.

He placed the lei over her head and looked into her eyes with an intensity stronger than he had ever used before. When he looked at her, it was as if no other woman had existed in the world before or ever would after. He let go of the lei and pulled away without kissing her.

But Teri felt as if she had been kissed—and kissed but good. The intimacy that had grown between them was much more powerful than anything she had ever experienced with a man. Yet aside from his hand on her shoulder after her "baptism" and the embrace in the crater, Gordon had never touched her.

Teri slid into the backseat beside her mother and remained silent as Gordon drove them back to Lahaina. He and Grandma kept up a lively conversation, and Mom kept saying how wonderful the flowers smelled.

"It's too bad you didn't get to see much of the island," Teri said.

"We'll have to come another time. I need to convince your father to come," Mom said. "He hasn't taken a real vacation in years. Once I get him here to see his granddaughter, I have a feeling he won't want to leave."

"Maui can have that effect on you," Teri said. "Now you can see why I've thought about moving here."

As they drove past the sugar cane fields outside of Lahaina, the sun was about to set in the late afternoon winter sky. Like busy little maids in waiting, the frilly white clouds gathered around the top of the Moloka'i mountain, preparing to tend to the sun before it made its way down the celestial aisle and gave itself to the ocean.

"I was wondering if you would allow me to treat you to dinner tonight," Gordon said.

"Oh, how thoughtful of you," Grandma said. "You don't need to do that for us."

"Well, to be honest, I've already done it." Gordon turned off the road into a gravel parking lot alongside the beach. It had a picnic area with tables, a restroom, outdoor showers, and a row of wind-bent coconut trees. He parked the car and came around to the passenger side, opening the door for Grandma and offering her a hand out. Then he opened the door for Teri and her mom. Gordon popped open his trunk and gathered in his arms all kinds of beach gear: a blanket, two folding beach chairs, an ice chest, and a guitar.

"Do you need some help there?" Teri asked.

"Could you grab those two shopping sacks? That ought to do it."

With his arms loaded, Gordon motioned with his head and said, "Follow me, ladies. Your sunset luau awaits you."

Teri started to giggle until it turned into an outright laugh. She sort of sounded like Gordon with his tickle-laugh. Everything had been so serious and so intense for the past week that this seemed crazy. She felt like a child being let out for recess in the middle of final exams.

They took the little path to the beach with extra caution. Perhaps Gordon was going slow for Grandma's benefit. Or maybe he was being cautious because of his tendency to trip, especially with his hands so full. A few people were enjoying the sunset on the beach, but not many compared to the beaches in front of the hotels and condos.

Teri had never been to this beach and thought it was a

beautiful hideaway. She had driven past it dozens of times but never guessed such a gorgeous strip of white sand stretched along the shore.

Gordon stopped in the sand and unloaded all his gear. He spread out the towels and set up a chair for Mom and a chair for Grandma. They were delighted. The man could do no wrong, as far as they were concerned. Teri placed the grocery bags alongside the ice chest and had a peek inside. A bag of marshmallows, a bag of taro chips, some hot dog buns, a bag of charcoal, and a roll of paper towels greeted her. This was going to be one unique luau.

"All right, ladies," he said. "I have some Hawaiian drinks for you here. Who would like papaya coconut?"

Grandma Maria cheerfully accepted the bottle of cold juice from the ice chest and set her sights on the evening sunset show going on directly in front of her. "*¡Que bonita!*" Grandma said. "What a perfect, perfect evening!"

"I only take you to the finest of dining establishments. Now, if you'll excuse me, I have to put the shrimp on the barbey, as they say." He pulled a package of hot dogs from the ice chest and grabbed the grocery bag with the charcoal and matches. "Help yourselves to those drinks there."

"Go help him," Grandma Maria said, nudging Teri.

"Help him what? He doesn't need me."

Grandma rolled her eyes heavenward and clutched her chest with her hand. "Oh, Teresa, of course he doesn't need you. But he wants you. This is a woman's dream."

Teri shook her head at her dramatic grandmother and reached into the cooler for a pineapple-mango juice. "If I didn't know better, I'd think you had a crush on that man," she teased.

"Well, at least one of us admits it!"

Positioning herself between her mom and grandmother, Teri sat down on the blanket with her back to Gordon. She hoped he hadn't heard any of their conversation. "What a beautiful sunset."

"Why can't you see that Gordon is the one man for you, Teresa?"

"Grandma, why are you even saying that? It would never work. He's nine years older than I."

"Your grandfather is seven years older than I."

"This is ridiculous! The man is from a different culture, he's different from me, and he came from a wild background. He doesn't fit my list of qualifications at all, Grandma."

"Perhaps you need a new list—like the one God wrote." Grandma Maria began to quote 1 Corinthians 13 in Spanish, stating how love is patient and kind and never jealous or conceited. Looking meaningfully at Teri, she completed the recitation with the statement that love never gives up.

Teri glanced over her shoulder at Gordon, who was several hundred yards away roasting the hot dogs. How could she tell her grandmother that she needed fireworks, and she wasn't sure there were fireworks with him?

Teri had to admit, even though he had never touched her, she felt as if he had with his eyes, if not with his hands or lips. The sensation those few times had been powerful.

Still, it was crazy. Her and Gordon? Never.

"You talk some sense into her," Grandma said, giving up and passing the baton to Teri's mom.

Mom's soft expression showed that she was on Grandma's

side before she even said a word. "I believe he would make you happier than you can even imagine. And I think you would make him the happiest man in the world. He's in love with you, Teri. It's obvious by the way he looks at you and the way he treats you. This is not the crush of a young boy. His is a solid, mature love that will make your heart sing, if you would open yourself to it."

"Did you two have a little conference with Gordon and set this all up?" Teri was beginning to feel trapped and annoyed that everyone had come to such conclusions about her life without checking to see what she thought.

"Of course not," Mom said. "When have we had time? This is the first we've talked of it."

"You both need to know one minor detail," Teri said, lowering her voice. "I'm not in love with him. Isn't that a prerequisite for marriage?"

Mom and Grandma exchanged sly smiles and nods.

"What?"

"Ever since you were a little girl, you were always the last to figure things out," Mom said softly. "Even though you can't see it yet, trust us: You are in love. Gordon is the one."

Now Teri was steaming. Feeling insulted by her mom's statement, she jumped up and strode down to the water, muttering all the way. "What do they know? Why do they think I can't see it? Meddling Mother. Nosy Grandma. Who asked them, anyway? This is my life, not theirs!"

What bothered her the most was that Mom had said, Gordon is the one. The day she had met him, when he had spilled Coke on her, Gordon himself had said, You may very well be the one.

234

She faced the bracing ocean breeze and silently shouted at God across the vastness. *What kind of joke is this? Everyone else has my life partner figured out but me? Would you make it clear to me if, by some odd miracle, he is the right man for me?*

Teri remembered praying this same sort of prayer on the beach during the early morning hours many months ago, only she was asking these questions about Scott. God had been silent that morning. He had not sent an answer on the crashing waves.

Nor did he send one this evening, either. The heavens kept their secrets once again, and all Teri could think of was how much she would like to run into the water right now, even with all her clothes on. She had gone in once before with her clothes on. When was that?

Oh, yeah. With Gordon. What is wrong with me? Here I am, trying to seek God's will, and all I can think of is going swimming with Gordon.

Then, as if a floodgate had opened, a number of thoughts about Gordon came gushing through: memories of their long talks in the crater, when Scott was too impatient to wait for her; the kind way Gordon had bought the lei for her at Kimos when Scott was too wrapped up in himself to notice she wanted it; and the way Gordon had never acted jealous even when it was obvious she and Scott were a couple.

Teri realized she had just gone through God's list of qualities in a fine husband, and Gordon had scored 100 percent. "Does he really love me, God?"

Teri knew the answer. Gordon had told her himself at Kimos when he was down on his knee. Why had she buried it so deeply that she had all but forgotten it?

Then she realized she had done that with other issues in her life. They always seemed to resurface, though. Deciding that the only way to figure this out was to think it through later, Teri headed back to the blanket. Tomorrow her mom and grandma would be gone. Once they were away from Gordon they would forget about him and stop needling her about him, too.

"Just in time," Gordon said as she settled herself back on the blanket. "We have a gourmet dinner ready here."

He had brought over half a dozen hot dogs skewered on a metal barbecue stick. Mom had opened the bag of buns and pulled some ketchup and mustard out of the ice chest.

"Great!" Gordon said. "What do you say we pray?"

Thirty-One

The leisurely luau could not have been any more perfect—except for the constant pounding of Teri's heart. She felt nervous, as if the group needed to get going, to move away from this mellow experience and return to the panic of the crisis over little Grace Malia.

"Are you going to serenade us now?" Grandma Maria asked the instant Gordon had finished his hot dog.

"Right," Gordon said, brushing off his hands and opening the guitar case. He tuned the guitar in the cool twilight and began to hum softly. A song rolled off his lips and floated past them on the evening breeze.

Teri tried hard to sit still, to pay attention and listen. The song was beautiful. But she couldn't keep herself from feeling jittery.

Still Gordon sang on. The song was about God, our heavenly Father, reaching out to his children. One of his arms was the law and the other was grace. The imagery switched, and the song described a lover reaching out for his true love. The arm of law and truth alone was not enough. The arm of grace and freedom was not enough. The Father could only draw his beloved child to himself when he encircled the child in a full embrace with both arms. The song's last line was about the lover holding out his arms, waiting to give that full embrace.

"What a beautiful song. The imagery!" Teri's mom looked overwhelmed. "I've never heard anyone explain it so precisely. 'God's Arms'? Is that what you called it? Where can I get a copy of this song? I would love to use it at our church."

"I suppose I could make you a tape," Gordon said.

"Do you mean you wrote that?" Mom asked.

Teri thought the song was beautiful, too. The picture it placed in her mind was a powerful one, one that cleared up something she had struggled with for years. Are we to live by rules? Or should we do what we want and depend on God to forgive us? The image of two arms being necessary for a full embrace answered that question. We need to live with both, not one or the other. Both.

Now Teri felt even more uneasy. She felt more vulnerable than she had allowed herself to feel in months.

"I think we should be getting back," Teri said, rising to her feet and cleaning up the food. "Anita and Dan are probably at the house by now, and they'll be wondering where we are."

"Oh, Teri, don't be such a nervous cat. Look at you!" Grandma scolded. "We can take our time here. Dan and Annie never come back before midnight."

"She told me earlier that they were going to leave after she fed Grace at six because she wanted to spend a little time with you two before you left in the morning."

"We can pack it up," Gordon said. He gathered the picnic

items together and helped Grandma Maria back to the car.

Mom and Teri walked behind them. Mom said, "Teri, if it helps you at all, I know your father would approve of him."

"Mother, you aren't listening to me! I'm not interested in a relationship with Gordon, or with anyone else for that matter. I'm happy being single."

Mom cast her a skeptical glance, and Teri looked down, wondering if she could convince herself of her own words.

She thought of Lauren. There, that was all she needed to renew her determination. Look at what had happened to her. And everyone thought Lauren and Jeff were perfect for each other.

Well, not everyone. Lauren's parents weren't thrilled with Jeff in the beginning. But they supported Lauren and her decision to marry him.

Dan and Anita were home, as Teri had predicted. They all gathered in the cramped kitchen quarters to talk. Then the door-bell rang.

They opened the door and a dozen friends from church stood there shouting, "Surprise!" In they came, a parade of people carrying baby clothes, a car seat, a white wicker bassinet, and a box full of casseroles ready to be frozen.

Mark and Claire were the last to walk in. Mark held a jumbo bag of disposable diapers. Somehow they looked a little out of place in his arms. Teri smiled at Mark and then at Claire.

"Oh, I didn't tell you," Anita said quietly, coming up behind Teri. "They were married the week before Christmas." She turned back to the man with the box of casseroles and said, "Yes, sure, the freezer is empty. Go ahead and put them in there. Thanks so much, you guys. This is great!"

"Hi," Mark said to Teri. "I heard you were here."

"And I just heard you two are married." Teri tried to cover her shock by extending warm wishes to both of them. "Congratulations! I didn't realize..." She didn't know what to say.

Mark slipped his arm around his glowing wife and said, "I guess I ignored the obvious for too long." Then he glanced back at Teri with a slightly apologetic look. "I mean, not that I would have wanted things to be different last year or anything..."

"I know," Teri said, leaning over to give him a quick hug. "You don't have to say anything, Mark. I understand, and I'm happy for you both." She hugged Claire too and said, "You know how it is with God. His timing and way of doing things are usually unpredictable."

"He's the wild one," Gordon said. Teri didn't know how long he had been standing next to her.

"That's for sure," Mark said. "The wild one." He reached over and shook Gordon's hand. "I haven't seen you since you got back. You know Claire, don't you?"

"Sure. Met at church a couple of times. Congratulations, Claire," Gordon said, stepping forward and giving her an aloha kiss on the cheek.

Funny how Gordon kisses everyone else, but he doesn't kiss me. Not that I want him to.

"So are you all finished with seminary?" Mark asked.

"Yes, I graduated three weeks ago and came right home to Maui. I'm praying about what the next step is for me."

"What are your options?" Mark asked, handing the bag of diapers to Grandma Maria, who was thrilled to be able to help Annie organize everything.

"I have an offer from a church in Sydney, but I'd rather stay here and start a new church. Maybe down in Kihei."

"That sounds great," Mark said.

"We need more pastors on the island," Claire added. "Especially pastors like you, who have such a strong heart for God."

Teri enjoyed being the silent one for once, just standing there and hearing everyone else give Gordon advice. She thought it might help redirect his thoughts.

"Well, if I stay, I think I'd be better at the task as a married man."

Teri felt her jaw clench.

"Gordon, buddy," Mark said in an uncharacteristically light tone, "now you're talking! I recommend married life highly." He slapped Gordon on the shoulder. "So have you found the lucky woman yet?"

Gordon didn't look at Teri but his words burned right through her. "I found her last summer. She's still trying to make up her mind."

That did it. Teri's mind *was* made up. She had told him once at Kimos, and she would tell him again a hundred times, if she needed to. *No! No! No! Gordon, I will not marry you.*

"Excuse me," Teri said, feeling her cheeks flush. "I'm going to see if Anita needs anything."

She fled through the crowded living room and retreated into the bedroom. Teri hadn't noticed that a man was there, assembling the bassinet.

"Teri, hi!" It was Kai, the poolside bartender who had gone on the crater hike with them.

"Hi, Kai. Hey, thanks for bringing this over and fixing everything up for Dan and Annie." She tried to sound light-hearted.

It occurred to her that everyone else was from church. What were Dan's work friends doing here?

"It's our pleasure. Jena and I are glad to help out."

"Jena? Have I met Jena?"

"Maybe not. She's my wife."

"Your *wife?*" Teri lowered herself to the edge of the bed. "Is it an epidemic around here, or what?"

Kai looked at Teri, the screwdriver still in his hand, and said, "Didn't Gordon tell you? He led Jena and me both to the Lord about two weeks after you left. We were baptized and married on the same day."

"By Gordon?"

"Yeah. Well, he assisted. It was at church with the pastor. Why do you look so surprised?"

"Oh, no reason. I'm glad, really! I'm especially excited to hear that you both became Christians. And you're married! That's great."

"Well, we'd been living together for almost two years, but once we were saved, we knew we needed to be right before God. It's been great. How about you? How have you been?"

"Fine." She was still startled by all of Kai's news.

"Hey, that was really something about Scott, wasn't it?"

Teri braced herself. "What's that?"

You know, how it turned out his roommate had stolen the *Moonfish.* You didn't hear all this?"

Teri shook her head.

"It was discovered by some guy who docked his yacht at Maalaea. They arrested Bob, but Scott got off because he was able to prove his innocence. He left the islands, though. Scott, I mean. I think he went to Peru. I saw Julie right before they left, and I'm pretty sure she said they were going to Peru."

"Julie? Bob's girlfriend?"

"Yeah, Bob's girlfriend until the police came knocking on their door. Then she quickly became Scott's girlfriend."

"I can't believe this," Teri said, dropping her head into her hands.

"Oh, that's right. You used to go out with him, didn't you? I forgot. I'm sorry."

"That's okay, Kai. That was a lifetime ago." Teri decided she needed some fresh air. She stood up and said, "Thanks again for helping out Anita and Danny like this. And again, I'm really happy for you and Jena. May God bless your marriage."

"He already has," Kai said with a crooked smile. "We found out two days ago that we're pregnant. I guess we'll be ready to borrow all this stuff right about the time they're done with it."

Teri bolted for the front door. *Babies! Marriages! Scott running off to Peru with Julie! I need out of here!*

Thirty-Two

Teri avoided contact with Gordon or anyone else for the rest of the informal party. It was all too much for her. It didn't make sense. None of it made sense. She stood out front and stared into the night sky. Six months ago, the stars had looked completely different. She thought of the night Scott took her to the beach and lit the fireworks. Her own words came back to haunt her: *The fireworks bit me.*

She realized that when she focused on the fireworks in a relationship, they were bound to turn around and bite her.

Okay, so I was wrong about Scott. I was wrong about Mark. Two failures are enough to make me not want to try again.

She heard the screen door open behind her. Teri stepped into the shadows and off to the side of the house. If it was Gordon, she didn't know what she would do. But it was Anita.

"Teri, are you out here?"

"Over here."

Anita joined her in the gray shadows. "Are you okay?"

"Why didn't you tell me Mark was married? Or about Scott?"

"Because I didn't know until tonight. Dan told me about Mark and Claire on the way home from hospital. I was just in the bedroom, and Kai told me about Scott. I'm sorry, Teri. What are you feeling?"

"Like I've blown it too many times."

"You haven't blown anything. You attempted several relationships, and they didn't work out. There's no shame in that."

"Maybe not shame," Teri said. "Maybe fear is what I'm fighting. My heart keeps pounding too hard; I'm all jittery."

"You're afraid to try again?"

Teri nodded.

Anita put her arm around her sister and said, "I know what you're feeling. I lost two babies. I was afraid to try again too. Afraid of what might happen. And look what has happened. It's not perfect. Gracie has a long way to go. But she's here. And I'm here. And God is with us."

Teri heard her sister crying softly, and she couldn't help but release her pent up tears and join in.

"I just want you to know," Anita said, wiping her tears, "that whatever you decide about Gordon or anyone else, I'm here for you. I want to be more than your sister, Teri. I want to be your friend."

They locked in a tight embrace, both arms wrapped around each other.

"Come on, let's go back in. I want you to help me find a place to put all these little baby clothes."

"Grace can have my old corner of the hall closet," Teri suggested.

They walked in the house, eyes red, and their arms around

each other. The group of friends were beginning to leave. Teri joined Anita in saying good-bye to each of them. Gordon left with the others, making a comment about how he would drive Mom and Grandma to the airport tomorrow morning at six. Teri felt relieved he didn't say anything else or give her one of his heart-to-heart looks. She felt too volatile right now. She needed time to think things through.

All night, as she lay on her futon bed on the living room floor, Teri's mind raced through a thousand different mazes. In the night's deep silence, she listened to the whirl of the ceiling fan and the soft snoring of Mom and Grandma, who shared the sofa Hide-A-Bed. Teri didn't sleep all night. But by the time the alarm went off at five, she had the answer she had been waiting for.

"Annie," Teri whispered, softly tapping on the bedroom door, "it's five. Are you guys up?"

"You can come in," Anita said. She was sitting up in bed, yawning. Dan, stretched out flat on his stomach next to her, was still dead to the world.

Teri tiptoed in and sat on the foot of the bed on Anita's side. "I need to tell you that I've decided to go home after all."

Anita's face fell.

"I was going to stay to help you get things together for the baby, but last night you pretty much received everything you needed. I also thought I'd be able to help with meals, but now your freezer is full. I need to leave. I don't have any more vacation time at work."

"I thought you said a terrific woman was subbing for you."

"She is, but if I don't go back, I might lose my job. You don't really need me here. I can't do anything for Grace Malia. The doctor even said that, since she seems to be stabilizing, all we can do is wait for her to grow. You don't need me here."

"But I'd like you to stay."

"I know but, Annie, try to understand. I need to go back to Glenbrooke where I can think things through."

Anita let out a sigh. "I understand. What are you going to tell Gordon?"

"I'll tell him to write me." Teri stood up. "I'm going to take a lightening fast shower. I'm already packed."

Anita reluctantly nodded. "Okay. I'll make some coffee."

Mom and Grandma weren't as understanding as Annie. Teri told them her decision as soon as she climbed out of the shower. They were still expressing their disagreement when Gordon arrived.

"Will you do something about this granddaughter of mine?" Grandma Maria said as Gordon lifted the three suitcases now returning to the airport.

"What would you like me to do?" Gordon asked, standing patiently by the front door. Everyone in the household was watching.

"I'd like you to get down on your knees and propose to her."

"Already did that," Gordon said without so much as a flinch in his expression.

Grandma looked shocked. She turned to Teri with her hands on her hips. "And what did you tell him?"

"Grandma, this is crazy. We need to get to the airport." Teri pretended to be fumbling in her purse for something.

"She told me no," Gordon said.

"And what did you tell her?" Grandma asked.

"I told her I would wait."

Grandma clucked her tongue, and with a wave of her hand in the air, she shuffled out to the car, muttering all the way in Spanish.

Teri refused to make eye contact with Gordon. She climbed into the backseat and remained silent all the way to the airport. As they reached Lahaina, Gordon twisted his rearview mirror so that with a glance he could catch Teri's face. She leaned closer to the window and looked out.

It ached to leave. She loved Maui. Yet to act on the admission that she loved anything or anyone…she just couldn't do it right now.

At the airport, Mom and Grandma checked in first since their flight to San Diego left twenty minutes before Teri's plane to San Francisco. Fortunately, Mom had a level head. She rattled off instructions to Teri about how she would box up all Teri's Christmas gifts, which were still at their home, and mail them to Oregon. Or maybe UPS them. She would check to see which was the better price.

"Okay, Mom. That's fine. Either one. I'll pay you back, if that would help."

"Don't be ridiculous. I don't want you to pay me back! Call us tonight once you're home, all right? We'll take turns calling here to get the update on Grace Malia, like we discussed."

"Okay, Mom." Teri bent her ear to listen to the flight being called over the loudspeaker. "That's yours," she said.

She kissed her mom and then leaned over to give Grandma Maria a kiss. Grandma returned a soft, moist one on Teri's cheek. Then grasping Teri's arm tightly, she said in a low, grumbling voice, "Don't be so stubborn."

"Grandma," Teri said, pulling away.

Grandma shook her finger at Teri and said, "You know what I mean."

Teri didn't know how to answer so she turned it into a joke and said, "And I love you, too."

Grandma kissed Gordon on both cheeks, and without a word she held his face in her two hands, looked into his eyes, and smiled.

Gordon smiled back, and then to Teri's surprise, he said to Grandma, *"Hasta."*

Where did he learn the Spanish word for "until"?

Grandma nodded her pleasure and agreement. *"Hasta,"* she repeated as if she needed no explanation for Gordon's farewell.

Mom gave him a quick kiss on the cheek, too, thanking him profusely for all he had done for them during the past week. "I imagine you'll be glad to get back to your job hunting now. We can never thank you enough for all you did."

"Was all my pleasure, really."

Mom and Grandma filed into line with the others boarding the plane and turned one last time to wave good-bye.

After they disappeared from sight, Gordon and Teri turned silently and headed to the end of the terminal hallway to wait for Teri's flight. They sat next to each other and gazed out the window at the wide-bodied jet that would soon be taking Teri away.

Finally Teri decided she must speak. But what should she say? Her heart had already been pounding. It only increased its rhythm, and her hands broke into a clammy sweat.

Gordon seemed calm, almost as if he were deep in prayer. No words came to Teri's lips.

Suddenly Teri's flight was called. She sprang up like a jack-in-the-box, her heart racing. "That's mine," she said.

Gordon walked with her to the rope divider that hung between the waiting room and the line of boarding passengers. He stood there like a rock. "I take it your answer is still no," he said.

"It would never work, Gordon. We're too different. I'm not ready for a serious relationship." Teri paused, trying to think if she had left out any of the reasons she had been feeding herself. She thought about her need for fireworks but didn't know how to explain that to him so she added, "And you're so much older than I. It's just not meant to be. Please try to understand."

Then, as if he hadn't heard a word she had said, Gordon stated, "I'll wait right here until it's a yes." He paused. "Until." He said the word firmly, not like a benediction but like a christening.

The line had moved ahead, and Teri needed to move with it. People were behind her, pressing her on. Gordon didn't make any move to hug her or touch her. She inched forward and looked at him over her shoulder. Their eyes connected, and in that mysterious way, as he had done before, Gordon's gaze drew her to him and embraced her.

Teri looked away. She had to remain strong. Clear headed. This was a wise, logical decision. It was the right decision. It had to be.

"Ticket please," the airline employee said at the door.

Teri handed it to her, received back the portion with her seat assignment, and walked toward the plane without looking back.

Thirty-Three

﹏❧﹏

Once Teri was seated with the seat belt fastened and the stream of air turned on and blowing right on her, she felt a little better. She knew she would be fine once the plane was airborne.

The rest of the passengers boarded. She flipped through the magazine from the rack in front of her. *Computer viruses are on the decrease. Well, that's good news. Travel clocks that can be programmed with your favorite wake up music.*

Teri jammed the magazine into the pouch and moved a little closer to the window as a passenger slid in and sat next to her. He was an older man who's broad girth filled the entire seat. When he sat, he let out a heavy puff, sounding quite exhausted from his journey down the aisle. Teri avoided looking at him. She didn't want to start a conversation. All she could think of was how hard it would be to get past him during the five hour flight when she needed to go the the bathroom.

She fished in her purse for some gum. Some mints. Anything. She had nothing. Without thinking, Teri started nibbling on her fingernails on her right hand. She nervously tapped her foot and droned out the flight attendants who were going through their spiel on emergency exits. The seat belt sign was on, they were ready for take off.

Come on! Come on! What is taking so long! Let's get going. Roll this baby down the runway, will you?

A full ten minutes passed and the captain's voice came over the loud speaker. "We are experiencing some back up here on the runway. This is not uncommon and we should be cleared to taxi to our runway in just a few moments. Please relax and keep your seat belts fastened."

Teri had nibbled all the fingernails off her right hand and was now starting on her left hand. Then she remembered Gordon asking her that morning on the beach if she bit her nails because that was one thing he didn't like. She nibbled with a renewed interest. What did it matter what Gordon liked or didn't like? She wasn't suppose to be thinking of him anyway. She was going home. Blocking him out of her mind. What was he doing here with her, so comfortably settled in her innermost thoughts like that?

She grabbed the magazine again and tried in vain to turn the pages with her stubby finger tips. *Why did I do that? Why did I bite off all my nails?*

Then, all of a sudden, the tears came. She couldn't stop them. Huge, watery drops ran down her cheeks and splashed on the magazine page.

This is crazy! Why am I crying? It must be all the stress from Annie and the baby and, and…I need a Kleenex.

Reaching under the seat in front of her for her purse, Teri rummaged around for a Kleenex, a piece of paper, or anything before her nose started to drip along with her out-of-control tear ducts. In the bottom of her purse she found an old, crumpled, and dirty pack of tissues with one last tissue in it. She fumbled to pull out the soiled tissue. It was stuck to the cardboard on the bottom.

With a tug, the tissue came out, along with a dried out object that fell on her lap. Teri blinked hard and tried to pick up the curious item. It was a pressed flower of some sort. She wiped her nose and turned the brown, squashed flower in the palm of her hand. It was an orchid.

Now where did I get an orchid, and why did I save it?

Suddenly a dam broke in her mind, and memories wildly spilled into her heart.

"Strange, isn't it?" she heard Gordon's voice whisper inside her heart. "The flowers don't resist blooming at their appointed time. Why do we?...I think four is good. I'd like even numbers. Six would be better than five...I could wait.... Does he embrace your heart with one arm or two? Answer that, and you'll know.... Frail humans we are, fumbling with the eternal...That great marriage feast of the Lamb.... I shall run into his open arms!"

The airplane began to roll back ever so slightly.

"Stop the plane!" Teri shouted at the top of her lungs. She released her seat belt, grabbed her purse, and yelled again, "Stop the plane!"

One of the flight attendants came rushing back to her aisle.

"I have to get out," Teri said frantically to the large man seated between her and the aisle.

"You can't get out now," he barked.

"I *have* to!" she hollered and crawled over the top of the man's knees, dragging her purse behind her. She was aware that every eye in this section of the plane was on her. She didn't care.

"Please take your seat," the flight attendant said, gently pressing her hands against Teri's shoulders.

"You don't understand! It's an emergency! I *must* get off this plane. Right now! Can't you just open the door and let me out? We haven't gone anywhere!" Teri sounded as frantic as she felt.

"But we've secured all the doors," the woman said.

Another attendant arrived and said, "It's all right. I received clearance from the captain. We can release her."

Teri bolted down the aisle, her hair waving wildly as she ran. Another flight attendant stood by the now open door and asked, "Do you require medical assistance?"

"No!" Teri shouted over her shoulder. She ran toward the terminal, her mind and emotions sprinting right along with her legs. She had left Gordon a full twenty-five minutes ago. He could be halfway home by now. She would get a cab. Or rent a car. Or hitchhike. She didn't care. She had to reach him.

The moment she burst into the waiting area, Teri stopped. Gordon was standing where she had left him. He hadn't moved an inch since his final words of, "I'll wait right here until…"

Teri stood frozen, panting hard, her eyes locked onto Gordon's. She said in one look with her eyes, everything that had been hidden so deeply in her heart for so long. He stood there, smiling, absorbing every bit of her message loud and clear.

Lifting both his arms toward her, Gordon invited Teri into his embrace. She ran as fast she could, wrapped her arms around him, and held him so close it felt as if her heart were beating in time with his. Neither of them let go.

"Gordon," she whispered, her tears soaking his shoulder, "I love you."

He drew back slightly and lifted his finger to brush the tears from her cheeks. "I take it then your answer is yes?"

Teri looked into his unflinching eyes. Tears brimmed on his eyelids. She remembered when he had proposed at Kimos and had told her the angels were watching. She could almost feel them now, hovering close, holding their breath, waiting with Gordon for her answer.

Teri whispered just loud enough for Gordon and the angels to hear. "Yes."

Slowly drawing her close, Gordon tilted his head, ready to give Teri the kiss he had saved for his one and only woman.

She closed her eyes. Gordon's lips met hers. And inside her heart it was the Fourth of July.

Dear Reader:

Above my kitchen sink is a wooden heart. It's painted blue with tiny yellow flowers. In white letters it says, "Na ke Akua Ke Aloha." My husband, Ross, bought it for me on our honeymoon in Hawaii eighteen years ago. We've been back to the Islands several times since then and even lived on Maui for a seven month stretch.

While working on this book I surrounded myself with pictures of Hawaii, listened to the island music and immersed myself in sweet tropical memories. It was torture because outside my window the gray, winter sky over Oregon refused to let the sun through and the leafless skeleton of an oak tree in my neighbor's yard shivered whenever the east wind blew through it. Maui seemed very far away. Swaying palm trees seemed like only a dream.

I feel that way about the Kingdom of God sometimes. I know it's real. I have proof. I believe. But the gray world around me refuses to let the Son shine through. It's like Gordon's line in this story, "Frail humans we are, fumbling with the eternal." One minute I boldly believe I understand God, and the next minute, he's shrouded with mystery and far beyond my comprehension.

Love seems to be the same way. I think I have it all figured out and then I blink and realize I don't know the first thing about how to love others or how to let others love me. How intertwined these two truths are: God and love. How endless their secrets.

Perhaps love enters our bleak days when we surround ourselves with its truth—no matter how far away it seems in our winter world. We believe the dream and as frail humans, we welcome

God's presence, his love, into our days—even at the risk of fumbling it.

The evidence of God and his endless love are all around us. We may not feel it in the earthquake, wind or fire of our difficult days. But it comes in a gentle whisper; like the words on the blue, wooden heart above my sink. "Na Ke Akua Ke Aloha"— "God is love."

Always,

Robin Jones Gunn

Robin Jones Gunn
c/o Palisades
P.O. Box 1720
Sisters, Oregon 97759

Palisades...Pure Romance

Refuge, Lisa Tawn Bergren
Torchlight, Lisa Tawn Bergren
Treasure, Lisa Tawn Bergren
Secrets, Robin Jones Gunn
Sierra, Shari MacDonald
Westward, Amanda MacLean
Glory, Marilyn Kok
Love Song, Sharon Gillenwater
Cherish, Constance Colson
Whispers, Robin Jones Gunn
Angel Valley, Peggy Darty (July)
Stonehaven, Amanda MacLean (August)
Antiques, Sharon Gillenwater (September)
A Christmas Joy, Darty, Gillenwater, MacLean (October)

Titles and dates are subject to change.

THE PALISADES LINE

Treasure, Lisa Tawn Bergren
ISBN 0-88070-725-9
She arrived on the Caribbean island of Robert's Foe armed with a lifelong dream—to find her ancestor's sunken ship—and yet the only man who can help her stands stubbornly in her way. Can Christina and Mitch find their way to the ship *and* to each other?

Secrets, Robin Jones Gunn
ISBN 0-88070-721-6
Seeking a new life as an English teacher in a peaceful Oregon town, Jessica tries desperately to hide the details of her identity from the community...until she falls in love. Will the past keep Jessica and Kyle apart forever?

Sierra, Shari MacDonald
ISBN 0-88070-726-7
When spirited photographer Celia Randall travels to eastern California for a short-term assignment, she quickly is drawn to—and locks horns with—editor Marcus Stratton. Will lingering heartache destroy Celia's chance at true love? Or can she find hope and healing high in the *Sierra?*

Westward, Amanda MacLean
ISBN 0-88070-751-8
Running from a desperate fate in the South toward an unknown future in the West, plantation-born artist Juliana St. Clair finds herself torn between two men, one an undercover agent with a heart of gold, the other a man with evil intentions and a smooth facade. Witness Juliana's dangerous travels toward faith and love as she follows God's lead in this powerful historical novel.

Glory, Marilyn Kok
ISBN 0-88070-754-2
To Mariel Forrest, the teaching position in Taiwan provided more than a simple escape from grief; it also offered an opportunity to deal with her feelings toward the God she once loved, but ultimately blamed for the deaths of her family. Once there, Mariel dares to ask the timeless question: "If God is good, why do we suffer?" What follows is an inspiring story of love, healing, and renewed confidence in God's goodness.

Love Song, Sharon Gillenwater
ISBN 0-88070-747-X
When famous country singer Andrea Carson returns to her hometown to recuperate from a life-threatening illness, she seeks nothing more than a respite from

the demands of stardom that have sapped her creativity and ability to perform. It's Andi's old high school friend Wade Jamison who helps her to realize that she needs inner healing as well. As Andi's strength grows, so do her feelings for the rancher who has captured her heart. But can their relationship withstand the demands of her career? Or will their romance be as fleeting as a beautiful *Love Song?*

Cherish, Constance Colson
ISBN 0-88070-802-6
Recovering from the heartbreak of a failed engagement, Rose Anson seeks refuge at a resort on Singing Pines Island, where she plans to spend a peaceful summer studying and painting the spectacular scenery of international Lake of the Woods. But when a flamboyant Canadian and a big-hearted American compete for her love, the young artist must face her past—and her future. What follows is a search for the source and meaning of true love: a journey that begins in the heart and concludes in the soul.

Whispers, Robin Jones Gunn
ISBN 0-88070-755-0
Teri Moreno went to Maui eager to rekindle a romance. But when circumstances turn out to be quite different than she expects, she finds herself spending a great deal of time with a handsome, old high school crush who now works at a local resort. But the situation becomes more complicated when Teri meets Gordon, a clumsy, endearing Australian with a wild past, and both men begin to pursue her. Will Teri respond to God's gentle urging toward true love? The answer lies in her response to the gentle *Whispers* in her heart.

Angel Valley, Peggy Darty (July)
ISBN 0-88070-778-X
When teacher Laurel Hollingsworth accepts a summer tutoring position for a wealthy socialite family, she faces an enormous challenge in her young student, Anna Lisa Wentworth. However, the real challenge is ahead of her: hanging on to her heart when older brother Matthew Wentworth comes to visit. Soon Laurel and Matthew find that they share a faith in God...and powerful feelings for one another. Can Laurel and Matthew find time to explore their relationship while she helps the emotionally troubled Anna Lisa and fights to defend her love for the beautiful *Angel Valley?*

Stonehaven, Amanda MacLean (August)
ISBN 0-88070-757-7
Picking up in the years following *Westward, Stonehaven* follows Callie St. Clair back to the South where she has returned to reclaim her ancestral home. As she works to win back the plantation, the beautiful and dauntless Callie turns it into a station on the Underground Railroad. Covering her actions by playing the role

of a Southern belle, Callie risks losing Hawk, the only man she has ever loved. Readers will find themselves quickly drawn into this fast-paced novel of treachery, intrigue, spiritual discovery, and unexpected love.

Antiques, Sharon Gillenwater (September)
ISBN 0-88070-801-8
Deeply wounded by the infidelity of his wife, widower Grant Adams swore off all women—until meeting charming antiques dealer Dawn Carson. Although he is drawn to her, Grant struggles to trust again. Dawn finds herself overwhelmingly attracted to the darkly brooding cowboy, but won't marry a non-believer. As Grant learns more about her faith, he is touched by its impact on her life and finally accepts Christ, and together they work through Grant's inability to trust.

A Christmas Joy, MacLean, Darty, Gillenwater (October)
ISBN 0-88070-780-1
Snow falls, hearts change, and love prevails! In this compilation, three experienced Palisades authors spin three separate novelettes centering around the Christmas season and message:
By Amanda MacLean: A Christmas pageant coordinator in a remote mountain village of Northern California meets a spirited concert pianist.
By Peggy Darty: A college ski club reunion brings together model Heather Grant and an old flame. Will they gain a new understanding?
By Sharon Gillenwater: A chance meeting in an airport that neither of them could forget...and a Christmas reunion.

PALISADES BACKLIST

Refuge, Lisa Tawn Bergren
ISBN 0-88070-621-X
Part One: A Montana rancher and a San Francisco marketing exec—only one incredible summer and God could bring such diverse lives together. *Part Two:* Lost and alone, Emily Walker needs and wants a new home, a sense of family. Can one man lead her to the greatest Father she could ever want and a life full of love?

Torchlight, Lisa Tawn Bergren
ISBN 0-88070-806-9
When beautiful heiress Julia Rierdon returns to Maine to remodel her family's estate, she finds herself torn between the man she plans to marry and unexpected feelings for a mysterious wanderer who threatens to steal her heart.